God's Grand Design

Booklet 3

Blessed Mother Mary

Reveals the Truth

About The Vatican

Richard Ferguson

God's Grand Design: Blessed Mother Mary Reveals The Truth About The Vatican by Richard Ferguson
Copyright © 2024 by Richard Ferguson
All Rights Reserved.
ISBN: 978-1-59755-834-1

Published by: ADVANTAGE BOOKS™
                       St Johns, Florida, USA
                       www.advbookstore.com

Unless otherwise indicated, Scripture quotations taken from The Holy Bible KING JAMES VERSION (KJV), public domain.

Scriptures marked (NKJV) are taken from the Holy Bible NEW KING JAMES VERSION®. Copyright© 1982 by Thomas Nelson, Inc. Used by permission. All rights reserved.

Library of Congress Catalog Number: 2024946291

Name: Ferguson, Richard, Author
Title: *God's Grand Design : Blessed Mothe Mary Reveals The Truth About The Vatican*
              Richard Ferguson
              Advantage Books, 2024
ID: ISBN: Paperback: 978159758341
Subjects: RELIGION & SPIRITUALITY - Catholicism

Evangeline Ferguson: Lead Contributor and Lead Editor

First Printing: November 2024
24 25 26 27 28 29 30   10 9 8 7 6 5 4 3 2 1

God Speaks To His Sacred Children about This Booklet And Its Author

"This Booklet is written for you by my special favored son. He is my sacred child, like of all of you are. But listen to what he has to say for I approve of his words in this booklet. He has worked very hard to bring you advanced truths of my creations. Richard is completely right when he describes that the spiritual realm, and the physical universe are indeed created so all of my sacred children may return to me after the rebellion of Lucifer and the fall of Adam and Eve as is described in your Christian Bible.

Listen to him with both your ears, for Richard has a unique and true understanding of things that are not available to those who believe in me by other means. I your Father in Heaven, have asked Richard to do something that I have never asked any others of my children. Listen to him for he is my Messenger, and he will help lead you back to me so we may together enjoy eternal life in a paradise that each of you can barely imagine. Yet, it is waiting for you.

Richard is one of my special children even before he was born on the earth. If you listen to what he has to say and read what he has written, that will lead you back to me without fail. I love all of you so very much from the bottom of my heart. Pray to me. Ask me questions about your lives. I will answer you. Be prepared to listen to what I have to say for it will be for your eternal goodness and salvation.

I love you, Your Loving Divine Father "

Table of Contents

Introduction

Firstly, writing this section of my previous book "God's Grand Design of All Creation for Your Redemption" from where this booklet is derived, writing it was the most painful, heart wrenching information I've ever wrote. Like the major book, in this booklet the Blessed Mother Mary reveals the truth of Our New Satanic Vatican in the End of Times. It was very painful for me to write about the reality that exists within the Vatican. And what Mother Mary told me all about the End of Times.

Yet, every sacred child of God who believes in Our Heavenly Father, our Lord and Savior Jesus Christ and the Holy Spirit must know this information. So as to be able to interpret the horrific events that started in the 1960s, continues to this day and will continue onward.

During the writing of this booklet a terrible event suddenly occurred where an assassin attempted to murder Pres. Donald Trump. Jesus Christ himself told me he wanted to tell me about that event. And instead of proceeding with this booklet in a normal manner, I am including the exact words of Jesus Christ that shed the absolute truth of what happened that day in Butler Pennsylvania. This will be chapter 1. Simply put, using one of my two angels that protect me that Angel deflected the bullet heading for the lower right skull of Donald Trump and would have killed him within a few minutes. Instead, my protective Angel deflected the bullet up to his upper for reasons Jesus Christ explains in the following section.

This introduction contains vital information regarding how this book came to be and the people involved in writing it. Unless you read others of my books, this will be the only sacred book besides the Bible that is in your possession. There are especially important points that must be made in this introduction so you will be able to understand the miracle you are holding in your hand.

1. 100% of everything you read in this book is completely true and is approved by your Almighty Father in Heaven. He is with me 100% of my life and knows all my thoughts and my

emotions and so on. I have been gifted by our Heavenly Father to be able to speak with Him, and also our Lord and savior Jesus Christ, the Holy Spirit and our Blessed Mother Mary. I am able to carry on conversations with the Trinity and Mother Mary. If I tell you something theological you can rest assured whatever I say is completely true. I have had a **Covenant of Truth** with our Heavenly Father for the past 40 years or so. I will not and cannot tell a falsehood in any of its forms.

2. Your author Richard Ferguson is indeed your **Heavenly Father's Anointed Messenger.** I was chosen by our Father for many reasons that are described later in this book. One of the reasons dates back to a conversation I had with our Heavenly Father while I was still in the Heavenly Kingdom before I was born to earth.

3. It was a monumental pleasure to have many different discussions with our Blessed Mother Mary in the writing of this book. We have come to know each other extremely well. To the point where at times I already know what our Blessed Mother is going to say. I wish all of you could hear her most unique and loving soft voice I have been gifted to hear in the writing of this book.

4. But when the writing of this book comes to an end, I will still always be able to speak with her and that gives me some Peace of Mind.

5. Lastly, contained within this book is detailed information about me and my spiritual life long before our Heavenly Father asked me to write, **God's Grand Design of All Creation for Your Redemption.** This book is the first of an increasingly long list of books that contain the information your heavenly father wants you to know about all his creations and how you fit into everything. It is a wonderful message of endless love and guidance coming directly from Almighty God that will lead you to heaven at the end of your life.

6. I owe it to you to document my spiritual history and abilities. So as to reassure you I am capable of performing the tasks Our Heavenly Father has asked me to perform on your behalf. Of this theological material out of my deep love for the Trinity and Blessed Mother Mary and especially for **_you_**, God's sacred children. Your Heavenly Father never makes mistakes, and he chose me to do this. I am completely honored and humbled he chose me.

7. I will not fail our Heavenly Father and I will not fail you his beloved sacred children.

8. One thing you should know, Satan has attacked me throughout my life. And while I am writing these theological materials your Heavenly Father wants me to; I am forced to perform spiritual warfare every day due to his attacks against me. Satan is a real pest.

ther details about me and my life in both the spiritual and physical realms later on in this book. In conclusion, the bottom line is I am a sacred child of God just like you. But in my case our Heavenly Father has chosen me to do some extraordinary things for the benefit of all others of his sacred children. And so, I will.

I love all of you sacred children ever so much,

Rich

1

The Unexpected Assassination Attempt on President Trump

Lord Jesus speaks to me about the Donald Trump Assassination Attempt

July 14, 6:00 PM.

My dearest son Richard, I wanted to explain a few things to you about the recent events yesterday and today in your country America. Yesterday, there was a legitimate and intentional attack against your presidential candidate Donald Trump. Your government knew about this coming attack and they turned their backs on what they knew was going to happen. This is one of your government's tactics. To manipulate the people, your father's sacred children, who live there.

The Democrat Party has actively and strongly promoted so many heinous sins against your heavenly Father. And what you said about the Democrat Party as my mother has said is that you are completely correct when you label them as the "Political Arm of Satan."

The fact that a rooftop with the clear view towards your next President, Trump, when he was speaking was allowed to happen is proof that your government purposely as you would say, dropped the ball. So as to allow this kind of thing happen with what your government calls, "Reasonable Deniability."

Yesterday, I mentioned to you, my dear son, that…. One of your angels instantly modified the trajectory of the one bullet that would have otherwise struck Donald Trump at the base of his neck on the right side higher into the cranial area. It would have killed him in a few minutes. But your angel deflected that bullet so it penetrated the base of his right ear as everyone knows now. What they do not know is that divine intervention saved literally your entire country from a horrific, grinding, and painful end of its history.

My dear son, normally we do not interfere with political events or the history of nations. Because all of that is a product of the gift of free will that your Father has bestowed upon all of his sacred children on earth. But in this case, there were only a few very guilty people high up in your government. Including your president Joe Biden and others that you know about like Hillary Clinton and a few others that gave secret orders to the Secret Police that you have posing as protectors of Mr. Trump.

Donald Trump will win the coming election in a huge landslide which will shift the political scene entirely in favor of the foundational principles, the Godly foundational principles, that your country was founded upon. Mr. Trump after he is in office, there will be many investigations to ferret out the criminals that have been so well entrenched in ever so many of your government branches.

The Communist sympathizers within your country will largely stop shouting so loudly and many of them will question what their political beliefs were. Our Father has seen the change of heart of so many of the citizens of the United States. Your Almighty Father wants to give your country another chance to avoid all the terrors and horrors of the End of Times as my Mother has described to you in great detail.

Europe, however, will continue to burn because of all the Muslims they allowed into their countries. As you know my dear son and have said many times, Islam is the religion of Satan. Of this there is no doubt for anybody that wishes to think about it in an objective manner. Both of us, you're Blessed Mother and I are so happy that your second major book is now in the publisher's hands. Advantage will do a very good job for you. Your friend and colleague, Mike will do everything proper. The next two or three booklets which you plan on publishing in the next three or four months is wonderful and please continue with that. Then I am looking forward to working with you and speaking together like we did on the first book to produce the third major book for people which is how to get back into heaven. And I know you're already thinking about the contents. As always, I will be at your side, along with your Blessed Mother.

I know you have a question in your mind. Please articulate it and I will answer.

Question: Thank you, dear Lord. Is there any one particular phenomenon or event that our Heavenly Father and You and the Spirit that influenced you to decide that United States would be given a second chance?

Answer: There were several things my dear son. We could see within the hearts of ever so many millions of people in the United States that they were rejecting more and more and more of the Communist Manifesto being perpetrated on them. In your country, more and more people were taking action to support the fundamental principles upon which your country was founded. Which, as we all know is based upon the rules of life set forth by your Heavenly Father. And we also knew that to release that beautiful energy into the social and cultural dimension of your country, it needed a spark of some kind. Which would ignite the pent-up passions and desires of your people for Almighty God to be expressed within your society. And take it away from the Marxist and Communist people that have thrived all too long in your culture and in your country.

It is now that, as you would say, my dear son, the worm has turned. In this case for the much, much better.

Question: My dearest Lord Jesus, would you feel it appropriate to name others that conspired in this assassination attempt please.

Answer: Of course, my dear son. The other names include Kamala Harris., the director of the FBI., the local Secret Service manager and the head of the Secret Service for the whole country. The local police officers and others that live in that small town knew nothing about this. It was the top people in the Secret Service that hatched this plan and ordered the higher-ups in that organization in collusion with the FBI to create this assassination attempt. In short there were approximately 12 people, all Democrats and Democrat appointees, who conspired to kill President Trump. Of course, my dear son the head of the FBI and one of his lieutenants were also directly involved. They then passed orders down their command hierarchy for some of their people not to do certain things that created the hole for the assassin to do his killing.

But, my dearest son, your Father and I decided to use one of your angels that protect you to deflect the bullet just enough so as to wound your next president very slightly. We knew this was necessary so as to demonstrate to your entire country the vile satanic nature of the Democrat party. There will be a flushing out of all the criminals that have infected the police, and security forces and your military forces in the coming few years. This will take time because as you always say dearest son, it takes only a little explosive to blow up a building but a lot of time and effort to rebuild it again.

God's sacred children who live in your country that believe in the holy Trinity and live their lives according to what your Heavenly Father has put forth deserve a second chance. Along with a further chance to spread His holy words of redemption which is exactly what is contained in those books you have already written and those still to come. And as you know my dearest of sons, you and your family are protected in the same manner that Pres. Trump has been and will continue to be.

I love you ever so much, my dearest of sons.

Thank you, my dearest Lord, and Savior Jesus Christ
I love you too!

2

Blessed Mother Mary

May 14, 2024

Blessed Mother Mary

Oh, my dearest of sons, how can I possibly thank you Enough. For working so very hard. And revealing to your Heavenly Father's sacred children ever so much of the content of what I have been trying to communicate to His children for the last 500 years or more. It has been, for me, extremely difficult and frustrating to bring forth the messages that our Father wants His sacred children to know about. As I have told you earlier, I have really had 375 apparitions each of which were intended to bring the love of your Almighty Father and the Trinity. But also tell this vitally essentially information, it is ever so sad for me to also have to bring the terrible warnings to God's children on earth.

As you know my dear son God's sacred children on earth are exposed purposely to Satan and all of his falsehoods and temptations. Each of you came to the earth to take what is known in the Heavenly Kingdom as the "earth test." This test has two features to it. The first is to experience your Heavenly Father in ways that go beyond what can be experienced in the Heavenly Kingdom. You will come to know your Heavenly Father in a far deeper and unique way than if you had chosen to stay in the spiritual realm in your home in the Heavenly Kingdom.

The second feature is you will be exposed to physical hardships and suffering on earth so as to evaluate your dedication and love for your Heavenly Father. Additionally, you will be exposed to so many different Satanic temptations that will include putting yourself above others of God's sacred children and even God Himself. Yes, you know dear son, this will lead people to their ultimate destruction in hell.

My dear son you have become far stronger within the spiritual Kingdom because of all the suffering you have gone through. And now you are God's Anointed Messenger to bring His message of peace, love, understanding and acceptance of the Godly rules that exist on earth. Also, dearest son you have done magnificently to explain to God's sacred children precisely how all of creation works and how it is tied together for the benefit of His sacred children.

Since I was born human on earth 2,000 years ago, I am able to bring much needed information to God's sacred children on earth. My messages of love can be found in my apparitions like the one at Lourdes. But even though it breaks my Heart, your Father asked me to bring messages of warning to His children on earth. This is because the large majority of His children have succumbed and given in to Satanic temptations. Most of them have abandoned Jesus Christ who is the way the truth and the life. No one goes to the Father except through Him. Over a period of time the children, on earth have rejected increasingly the one true God. And have fallen for physical sensual pleasures, adoration of Pagan Gods and given up true Godly morality replacing it with their imaginary rules that are invented so as to bring physical pleasure only. Once my dear son you have described the country you live in as a modern-day Sodom and Gomorrah.

You are so right dear son. Ever so sadly dear son, you are also so very right when you said that your Democrat party is the political arm of Satan. If only people could stand back and look at what has been happening to your society through them and where the tragic events will continue to occur because of them. The destruction of your southern border is one example where tremendous pain and suffering is now just starting to happen to your society. Such that your country will become unrecognizable from every other sad country in the world just like what your former President Barack Obama has wanted. I remember dear son he said, "I see no reason why America should be any better than all the other countries in the world." Look to Canada and the tragedy unfolding there which is what will happen to your country if you do not turn to God.

It is for these reasons that I have come to earth and appeared to many people 375 times. So as to plant the seeds of Godly love to everyone who is willing to listen and live their lives accordingly. Because of my efforts and the unwillingness of people today to spread my words of love. And importantly of the warnings of what will come if they continue to turn their backs on the one true God, there will be many catastrophes from many different directions on earth.

Dear son, you have documented my warnings very well inside this book. And all the time and the efforts and the suffering you have gone through to bring this book to God's sacred children. The same milestone of love of you for your Heavenly Father and the Kingdom of Heaven.

The only last thing I can say is I look forward so much to hug you and thank you upon your arrival within the Heavenly Kingdom.

I love you ever so much,

Your Blessed Mother Mary

Thank you, dear Blessed Mother Mary! I love you too ever so very much! We will always continue our discussions.

3

Blessed Mother Mary Reveals Truths Never Heard Before

Yes, our Blessed Mother Mary does indeed speak directly to me regarding the topics in this sacred document. Over the years since the life of our Lord and savior Jesus Christ, Blessed Mother Mary spoke to many people and had many apparitions to a wide variety of people in the years since then. In fact, Mother Mary has appeared 375 times to various people across the world, far more than you have been led to believe. She has also had an ongoing relationship with Pope John Paul II as seen another example. Our Blessed Mother Mary will always choose to speak with selected dedicated Christians that love the Holy Trinity and of course Blessed Mother Mary herself.

Our Blessed Mother Mary has chosen to speak to me because your Heavenly Father has asked me to be His Anointed Messenger. My mission is to bring all of His sacred children His message of love, peace, acceptance. And advanced theology that brings far deeper understandings of not only the Trinity but also His creations and why they all exist. You can find that information in another book I have written last year in 2023 titled, God's Grand Design of All Creation for Your Redemption.

My dear sacred children of God, this book you are holding in your hands is no ordinary book. It is a sacred document. Why? It is approved by God Our Heavenly Father and Blessed Mother Mary. It is sacred because it contains the direct words of our Almighty Heavenly Father and our Blessed Mother Mary. The contents of this book are in perfect alignment with our holy Bible. There are no incompatibilities. It centers around the magnificent apparitions of our Blessed Mother Mary and her messages to all of God's sacred children on earth. In very many ways Mother Mary is the link between the Heavenly realm and the physical realm on earth.

This book contains a selected number of Mother Mary's apparitions that apply very directly to the end of times that the earth has entered into. Signs of the End of Times are all over the earth if anyone cares to pay attention. This book will explore the prophecies made by our Blessed Mother Mary and how at this time they are increasingly being fulfilled. There have been all too many charlatans in the media claiming they know what is going to happen. A very few holy people do but the vast majority just want to sell you something. The very first part of this sacred document we'll focus on Mother Mary's apparitions at Fatima Portugal.

It is her apparitions at Fatima, especially the third secret, that directly apply to the state of the world we are experiencing now. It is her apparitions from Fatima that the Catholic Church tried to keep secret. This is because the truth of what Mother Mary had to say revealed awful Satanic things about the Catholic Church. Other apparitions we will discuss support Mother Mary's words in Fatima.

All sacred words Of Blessed Mother Mary contained within this book will always be presented in bold and italicized print. My words as your faithful Anointed Messenger and author will always be in regular Times New Roman text.

On page 2, you have read the exact words of our Heavenly Almighty Father spoken to me as a message to all of His sacred children. This means you. Not only does this book bring the message from Almighty God, a message of love, of understanding, acceptance, and advanced theological understandings as revealed by our Blessed Mother Mary.

The contents of this sacred book will indeed shock many of you. Much of the content of the secrets of Fatima is very upsetting yet we have been living in the beginning of the end of times since 1960. Lately Pope Francis claimed he "finally revealed the entire contents of the third secret of Fatima" Pope Francis is a damned Satanic liar. Included later within this book are the Pope's so called total revelation word for word. After that are the exact words of our Blessed Mother Mary who revealed the third secret to the three shepherd kids at Fatima. Sister Lucia is the child that wrote down Mother Mary's words. They DO NOT match with Pope Francis at all. More on that later.

Most Christians think of our Blessed Mother Mary as the Mother of God and who appears on occasion in apparitions with children emphasizing the need for prayer, sacrifice, penance and praying the rosary.

I am fortunate enough to be one of the people Our Blessed Mother Mary wishes to talk to. In my case it is for writing the books that contain the messages of our holy Father in Heaven, our Lord and Savior Jesus Christ and of course our Blessed Mother Mary.

As our Father's Anointed Messenger, it is my holy mission to bring God's truth of all creation to you His sacred children. I will do this until as Jesus Christ told me, until I rejoin Him in the Heavenly Kingdom. The following text explains in some detail how I became our Heavenly Father s Anointed Messenger. The process of becoming the Anointed Messenger started before I was born to this earth.

Now, in everything I say and write, the question will always remain why I should believe this author and what he says Mother Mary told Him. The answer to that question is really quite simple. I ask you to pray directly to our Heavenly Father our lord and savior Jesus Christ and the holy spirit which proceeds from them. Ask them if what you are reading is true and correct. I am God's Messenger not God's sales associate. All I can do is to tell you the truth about the Trinity and

Mother Mary says. I am not here to try and convince you of anything. Our Heavenly Father gave you free will and a magnificent capacity for logic, reason, and faith. If you use the tools Our Heavenly Father gifted each of us with, you will come to understand everything within this book and the others I have written are true.

I am our Father 's messenger and I will not engage in Christian apologetics. From the sacred words I bring, you will either come to a higher level of understanding and faith, or you will reject it. I always remember what Saint Thomas Aquinas said many years ago:

If You Have Faith and You Believe, No Proof Is Necessary
If You Don't Have Faith and Disbelieve, No Proof Is Possible

If you have questions or are confused about something within this book, I strongly encourage you to pray to Almighty God about that. It is in this way you can never ever go wrong. Remember as I described in the first book of this series titled, Our Heavenly Father loves each of us so very much. So as when we were created in the blink of an eye billions of years ago in the Heavenly Kingdom, he left part of Himself within our personal spiritual being. It is in this way Our Heavenly Father knows everything about us and will always hear every prayer we ever say. He has promised each of us he will always answer every one of our prayers and questions.

My Anointed Messenger History. Who Exactly Is Your Author of This Book?

I think it is necessary at this point to document for you who I really am. I cannot go into tremendous detail because this book is about our Blessed Mother Mary and not me. It is only fair I reveal to you not only who I am but also my background and my activities throughout the life I lead. This also includes some personal items and my educational background as well.

I was born to earth as an only child. I was not wanted by either of my parents. To them I was just an irritating obstacle. My father was a violent man, and my mother never lifted a finger to stop Him from beating me for the slightest transgression as a small little boy. Years after leaving home, Jesus told me my father was there to do everything he could to stop me from fulfilling my life's mission as agreed to between me and our Almighty Father in Heaven. Satan wanted to destroy me through the cruelty of my own father. Satan failed and my father is now in hell because of what he did to me and many other horrible things. Even if you have not had experiences like this do NOT make the mistake, they are not true. I went through public school then got accepted to Santa Clara University where I got bachelor's degree in chemistry and physics with minors in philosophy and theology. I had a job pumping gas at a gas station in San Jose so I could and pay for half my tuition. Later I got a job at IBM doing computer maintenance.

Upon graduation I had a choice to make. Since I had a commercial pilot's license, I obtained on the side I could have a wonderful career with the airlines. Or I could have a more settled life working for NASA as a research scientist at the Ames Research Center. I ended up working for NASA as a scientist exploring upper atmospheric particles that arrived at the earth from interstellar space. This gave me enough money to pay the tuition to get a master's degree in business. Loving flying as I do, I was a flight instructor on the side. Over the years I've owned three different airplanes along the way.

Over the years I found myself developing a small real estate investment company that allowed me to retire in my 50's.

During my late 40's I started to feel and ever-increasing yearning in my life to know God far better than I did. Every day I felt this increasing emptiness within me I knew only Our Heavenly Father could fulfill. By then in my life a number of spiritual events have already occurred. This supported my growing need through fundamentally "come to God." At the time I worked in corporate computer marketing for Hewlett Packard corporation. I had a travel schedule worldwide. This conflicted with my class schedule. But the university was very accommodating, and this gave me the opportunity to work extremely hard to receive another master's degree in pastoral ministry and theology. My chosen minor was spirituality. Over the coming few years after graduation, I wrote six Christian spiritual books. You are reading book nine.

When I started to write book number seven, something miraculously occurred after I got through the text to page 20. <u>My world completely changed at that point</u> I had absolutely no idea of.

By then in my life, I already had numerous spiritual experiences. I did not know it at the time, but I was already on Satan's radar screen. This is because there are no secrets in the spiritual realm and my identity is known to everybody in the spiritual realm. This includes Satan. Satan also knew of my previous discussion with our Heavenly Father before I was born to the earth. Because of Satanic influence it is my father who did everything he could when I was growing up to destroy me. He wanted to mold me into his own Satanic image. It did not work. Lastly, on him, my father is indeed in hell as he tried to come up from under the floor to me four times. And each time, I told him to go back to hell where he belongs in the name of our Lord and Savior Jesus Christ. Speaking of this all Christians should know you have authority over Satan. Just tell them to go back to hell in the name of our Lord and savior Jesus Christ. Then say one Our Father and Hail Mary and thank our Father in Heaven for your power over Satan.

I later found out from Jesus I had a conversation with our Loving Father in the Heavenly Kingdom about my coming life on earth. That discussion determined my life theme when I was born to the earth. My life theme is amazingly simple. I wanted to put every other one of God's sacred children ahead of me and I would serve them. I would serve others of God's sacred children by bringing advanced understandings of our Father 's creations to them. However, Jesus Christ pointed out to me that this is one of the most difficult life themes for sacred children coming to earth. Satan hated this. One point of education for you about the spiritual realm is that there are no secrets whatsoever. Everybody knows everything about everybody else. Please ponder this.

Satan Attacked Me Viciously Three Times

This is something Satan hated terribly about me, and he would want to destroy anybody that has such a loving God centered theme in their earthly life. <u>The one most terrible experience I had was when Satan attacked me three times in the middle of the night</u>. This occurred on three separate occasions. There was a loud crash within the house as if a car crashed through my home and into the living room.

When Satan invaded my bedroom where my wife and I sleep, and our two children in the next bedroom, I thought all hell broke loose with the most horrific crashing sound I could ever imagine. When I looked up toward the foot of the bed there stood Satan Himself. Remember Satan can be only one place at a time. And there he was standing at the foot of our bed staring at me with his glowing red eyes.

There is no doubt it was Satan. To picture what he looked like, start with the Star Wars character Darth Vader. His voice had a certain deep quality to it with horrific anger and rage that just cannot be duplicated by any human being. He stood about seven feet tall. He outstretched His arms to almost 90° with His attached blackest of black cape that covered a lot of material. Standing at the foot of my bed he bent over, and his hooded eyes and head were staring right at me. By the way, His eyes are indeed a very bright terrifying red.

With that and His body bent over such I had to look up almost vertical to see His head and red eyes. Then he yelled at me these words, "at the top of His ugly voice he yelled at me three times. He said" **<u>I will get you! I will get you! I will get you!"</u> <u>After yelling this at me with his booming loud voice when His head was no more than two feet from my nose, he leaned backward to straighten Himself. He continued to stare at me for some more seconds. Then with the audible whoosh he departed my bedroom to the left. He went straight through the wall as if it did not exist. Silence and peace returned to our bedroom.</u>**

Yes, I was completely frightened by this. But I did not pee my pajamas. Okay, that's a manly thing. However, in the succeeding weeks and months I learned about spiritual warfare. I learned Satan and His demons can be controlled by true Christian believers. It is not that hard, and they must obey. Since then, I have been forced to conduct spiritual warfare every day.

The Beginning of My Christian Spiritual Warfare

Since then, Satan has harassed me every day of my life. When I'm writing the sacred books our Heavenly Father wants me to write for His anointed children, Satan would be there throwing rotten thoughts into my brain so as to distract me and conduct harassment. I was forced to conduct spiritual warfare.

I must tell you this dear sacred child of God, to battle Satan is not as hard as you think. Is it scary? Yes at least at the beginning. But after a while it gets to be routine. If you are on good terms with our loving Father, our Lord and savior Jesus Christ and the Holy Spirit which proceeds from them it is relatively easy. Every time when I am writing and Satan tries to interfere, I just simply stop what I am doing calmly then I say one Our Father and one Hail Mary. Then I command Satan to leave me, to depart me and go back to hell where he belongs in the name of our Lord and savior Jesus Christ and our Blessed Mother Mary. Satan must obey otherwise he will get chopped up into a fine powder by one of God's archangels. One time the Angel that appeared to do this asked me if I wanted to watch. I said yes.

At the beginning I saw Satan and then the Angel started to do His work with His sword. Shortly thereafter that all I saw were tiny bits of Satan's body strewn all around the place. His body color is also a red maroon kind of tint to it. The Angel said it would take Him a long time to reconstruct Himself. Frankly, me being me, I wanted to set fire to that pile of body fragments and perhaps have a weenie roast. Nonetheless this gives you an idea of my life as I pursue with love, deep love and devotion to the Holy Trinity and our Blessed Mother Mary. Satan is not to be feared but do not get careless either. I would rather he be ordered back to hell where he belongs for, he must obey the commands given by a sacred child of God in the name of our Lord and savior Jesus Christ.

What I just told you also applies to non-Satan personages as well. My father was a very cruel person, and at times after he died, rise up from the floor. And in a very harsh tone of voice say to me, "I want to talk to you." My response was simply, "go back to hell where you belong in the name of our loving savior Jesus Christ." He had to obey, and I could physically see Him descend back down through the floor and then the episode was over. My Father being in hell is exactly where he should be.

That being said a summary of my life as told to me by our Lord and Savior Jesus Christ started when I was still in the Heavenly Kingdom before born to this earth. I had a conversation with our Heavenly Father. After I was born to the earth to two parents that did not want me, I made it through bachelor's degrees and then master's degrees in business. At NASA I enjoyed interacting with the U2 spy plane which carried particles filters up to 80,000 or 85,000 feet where they could collect upper atmospheric particulate matter to determine the constitution of interstellar particles. After that I had a normal career in corporate computer marketing at Hewlett-Packard corporation. I raised three children before my late wife died of cancer. However now I am so happily married to a beautiful woman that one point in her life taught theology at the university of Santo Tomas in Manila Philippines.

This book is a must read for all Christians and all people who believe in Almighty God. It is perfectly consistent with our beloved Biblical literature. However, it explores advanced theology our Father wants all of His sacred children to understand. Additionally, it brings to everyone His message of love and acceptance. He wants ALL His sacred children just how much He loves them and wants to pursue them so they will say "yes, I want to go back into the Heavenly Kingdom from where I came.

This book is number 9. Number 8 is a book about creation in all its detail. Both of these books are based on our existing Biblical literature and information articulated by our loving Lord and savior Jesus Christ and our Blessed Mother Mary. Everything I write is completely consistent with both the Old Testament and the New Testament. But they go far beyond the Biblical understandings and bring magnificent more detailed understandings of how all of God's creation works together which includes all of His sacred children living within His creations. More booklets are coming that will expand everyone's deepest understandings of so many distinct aspects of Almighty God and His creations and how they all fit together for the benefit of you, His sacred children.

The Unexpected Arrival of Jesus Christ and Blessed Mother Mary

When I was approximately 70 years old, I was meditating after I got up and swung my feet over the side of the bed. I noticed something very strange occurring about forty feet away in front of me. There were two spiritual entities there just standing there and looking at me. It was easy to see that one was a male with brown hair and white robes. The other person was definitely female with blue and white robes and a blue hood over the top of her head. She was shorter than the male. The first time I saw this having been experienced at seeing other spiritual beings, it was not that big a deal to me, but it got my attention. After a few seconds I went about my business for the day. The next day I woke up and I noticed these same two spiritual persons looking the same but being a little closer to me than the previous day before.

Well, that got my attention. Something was up but I had no idea what it was. But I had things to do, and I resumed my daily activities. On the third day when I woke and swung my feet over the right side of the bed, these two spiritual persons were still even closer than the previous night and the one before. They still remained silent but now I knew something was really up, but I did not know what. On the fourth day they were no more than five or six feet from me in front and to my right side. Strangely I was almost certain I knew who they were at this point, but I did not dare say anything, at least not yet. I was beginning to think these two spiritual people were Jesus Christ and our Blessed Mother Mary. Naw, that cannot be or so I thought.

Now the fifth morning arises. It was a morning like no other in my entire life. When I woke up laying down and staring at the ceiling, I did not see them. I wondered where they went. Soon I was to find out in a matter of seconds. When swinging my legs over the side of the bed, the gaze of my eyes caught the unmistakable image of our Lord and savior Jesus Christ and our Beloved Blessed Mother Mary. They silently stood right next to my right shoulder. Perhaps 4 to 6 inches away from me. This shocked the heck out of me. I did not know what to do, I did not know what to say, I did not know anything to do in any way. I was completely stunned. There I was, my feet hanging over the side of the bed with two Biblical sentient spiritual beings standing right next to me on my right side.

I started to go into a state of shock. But I had enough presence of mind to ask the following question in a telepathic way I have used many times before speaking with spiritual beings: I asked, "**are you who I think you are?**" Jesus answered with these exact words, "**_Yes, it Is I._**" Instantly I thought it strange he did not say "it is me." Because that is the incorrect English everybody uses. Proper English is exactly what Jesus said." **_Yes, it is I_.**"

With that response from Jesus, everything and I mean absolutely everything within all of my senses turned completely white. All my surroundings in the bedroom completely disappeared. They were gone. I no longer felt I was sitting on the edge of my bed. There was no sensation at all. The ceiling was gone, the floors were gone, the bed I was sitting on was gone. The only things that existed were my consciousness, my identity, and an awareness of who I was with and where I thought I was but apparently not anymore. Instantly, the only awareness I had was I existed, and our Lord and savior Jesus Christ and Mother Mary were close by my right side. There was nothing else. There was absolutely no fear.

The next thing I heard was dear Lord Jesus telling me to put my feet back up on the bed and just rest and remain calm as much as I can. I did that, but in the process, I didn't see my legs anymore. I don't remember feeling them either, nor did I see the rest of the bed or the rest of the bedroom for that matter.

It was just me, our loving Lord Jesus Christ, and our beloved Mother Mary. Nothing else!

After an unknown time resting on the bed. Jesus told me to just keep laying down and listen to what he wanted to tell me. He said Mother Mary and He are there to help me with the coming things our Heavenly Father wants me to do for the rest of His sacred children on earth. I do not remember His exact words but that is the central idea.

Jesus also told me both He and Mother Mary would stay with me by my side forever more. They will never leave me. I felt wonderful hearing that.

After this encounter, our Lord, and Savior Jesus Christ and Our Blessed Mother Mary were indeed at my right-hand side 100% of every waking moment of my life. I can see them in full living color. They are with me always, and they know absolutely everything about my existence, including what I was thinking, what I was feeling, what was happening to me and everything else directly associated with my existence. Today they remain indeed always with me by my side. There was never a moment when I couldn't see them, but rather I can always see Jesus with our Blessed Mother Mary in her blue and white robes, and our Lord and savior Jesus Christ. To this day as I write this sentence, I can clearly see both of them standing no more than six inches from my right shoulder.

Frankly at first this whole thing was quite unnerving. But after a while I started asking Jesus a lot of questions about so many different theological topics. He is always ever so happy to answer anything I wanted to know. It is through this personal tutoring of our Lord Jesus I learned ever so much about creation and about all the details related to how creation works together through its individual facets of existence.

Hint: all aspects of our Heavenly Father's creation work together like all the parts of a fine Swiss watch. They mesh together perfectly for one reason and one reason only. All of creation exists for the sole purpose of God's sacred children making their way back to the Heavenly Kingdom from where they came.

Secondly, it is to provide His sacred children the opportunity to choose either our Father or Satan. We make this choice by how we conduct our lives.

It is through the private tutoring of our Lord and Savior Jesus Christ along with our Blessed Mother Mary that has given me the most magnificent information. All about creation both in the spiritual realm and the physical realm that allowed me to write the master book **_"God's Grand Design of All Creation for Your Redemption."_** I didn't rely on any other resources, like online or YouTube because why do that when Jesus Christ is the one that did indeed create the entire physical realm, we call the universe.

Why Me Lord?

During the time I was writing that book, this question came to me. After a while I began to wonder, "why me?" Why did our Heavenly Father choose me out of all the others of God's sacred children within the universe. To ask, of all people, to be the anointed messenger and write this ever so important book? The most important book that will become recognized as a sacred book in the eyes of the Christian community along with the Old Testament and the New Testament.

I asked Jesus that exact question. **WHY ME?** Jesus once told me sometime last year our Heavenly Father chose me to be His Anointed Messenger because of <u>something I said to Him</u>. First dear sacred children of God, all of you were in the Heavenly Kingdom BEFORE you came to earth. All of us could talk with our Heavenly Father. Well, that really got my attention. What on earth could I possibly have said? And the other thought I had was, "oh good grief, me and my big mouth!" Sometimes I tend to do that.

Yep. That was my instantaneous thought when Jesus told me that. After I gathered myself a little bit, I asked our Lord what did I say? Jesus told me that before my upcoming earthly life I told our Heavenly Father I wanted to put other people ahead of myself while I was in my upcoming life on earth. This would be my lifetime theme as all of us do have a life theme. Jesus then told me that this is a particularly difficult life to live. Boy, was he right! Maybe I will write an article about that. At this point though I think I should terminate anymore thoughts about how I became our Heavenly Father's Anointed Messenger. I have already spent too much time away from our Blessed Mother Mary.

There is one thought I wish to leave you with. Regarding my lifetime on earth as a chosen one, I know our Heavenly Father is within me just as he is within every sacred child of His on earth. This means YOU! Yes, you, as everybody are a sacred child of Almighty God. All sacred children are made in the image of God. This is why Satan hates every one of us. If you were a rabbit, he would not care. In an upcoming book, I will describe the trials and tribulations in my life caused by hateful Satan against me because he knew our Father chose me as His anointed messenger.

Regarding our Blessed Mother Mary, it was she and our Lord and Savior Jesus Christ that approached me some years ago now. They told me they would be with me forever by my side. My dearest sacred children of God, I cannot begin to tell you how magnificent it is to see Lord and Savior Jesus Christ and Blessed Mother Mary right beside me slightly behind my right shoulder. And yes, dear sacred children I can see them in living color.

This is why at certain points of this book centering upon our Blessed Mother Mary, you will read her saying things. Certain things pointing to Her instantaneous knowledge of how I am physically feeling, how tired I can get and many times becoming exhausted. Even though our Mother Mary is now a pure spiritual being, she retains the ability to know and understand my feelings within my physical body.

Question: Dearest Mother Mary, during the time you and Jesus were approaching me for the first time would you comment please on what it is you were thinking about all of that? Jesus did do all the talking and I would really like to know what your thoughts were as a you and my savior approached me for the first time.

Answer: *Of course, my dearest son, I felt this certain amount of trepidation because we did not know exactly how you would react. We know your love for your Heavenly Father and Jesus, the Holy Spirit and me was very great. But we needed to be very gentle with you because the last thing we wanted was to in some way as you would say "scared the pants off you." You have had many spiritual experiences in your life already before we approached you. And that was an exceptionally good thing. Because of your experiences that ranged from the elders on the cruise ship praying for your late wife Marilyn to Satan Himself trying to scare the living daylights out of you. There were so many other incidents that we felt this would be one more spiritual experience for you that would not damage you in any way.*

This is what we were very afraid of with any sacred child of God still living in their physical body.

It was your love for God and for me that made me feel you are the only right person. With all your experiences academically with your degrees in chemistry and physics and being a pilot, which demands certain amount of perfection and discipline. And the way that you brought up your children within the Catholic faith and their education. And that you are the leader of your family bringing them up in the right way. Along with then you getting your master's degree in ministry and theology we knew that you had all the necessary qualifications to do what it is your Heavenly Father has asked you to.

I felt strongly that you would say yes to your Heavenly Father. So too did Jesus my son. I will never forget before Satan attacked you those three times when you were yelling at Him for making a mess on earth that you repeated those terrible swearwords aimed at Him. It showed us that you were just not afraid, and you were a fighter. When our Heavenly Father joined you on the airplane. When you were halfway across the Pacific Ocean. And He told you that he was happy you were a fighter right after Satan attacked you in your airline seat, you just reconfirmed everything we thought that you would become. And you have become everything we wished for plus a lot more.

It is particularly good that you asked me this question. Because all these sacred children of your Heavenly Father when they read this will understand just how close all of us are together. Which includes everyone of God's sacred children also as you have demonstrated throughout this book many times. I love the fact that you speak your mind in truly clear forceful terms. And in addition to you being a fighter you also have all the protections of the Heavenly realm right by your side.

My dearest of sons I love you so very very much. And, in a way, I hope that we can just keep writing and writing and writing this book, but I know it must come to an end sometime soon. But I will always be with you right by your side along with my son for that is timeless and will never end.

I love you dear son, Your Mother Mary

Each of us are really two parts. The physical part and the spiritual part. The physical part is what dies after 70 or 80 years. The spiritual part is eternal. The reason our Blessed Mother Mary could keep track of how I'm feeling during the writing of this book is because my spiritual part is connected to my physical body. And that is how our spiritual Blessed Mother Mary knows how I am feeling, what I am thinking and how tired I get at times. We both have a deep spiritual connection with each other. My dear sacred children of God, I cannot begin to tell you how wonderful that is.

For me, the same connection is also true with our Lord and Savior Jesus Christ. Needless to say, this also includes our Almighty Loving Father. Both Jesus and I along with our Heavenly Father do speak with each other as we wish. If you want to learn more about these sacred connections, my first booklet titled "God's Grand Design, Booklet 1, Creation".

If anybody that tells you that you are nothing more than a pile of chemicals that started out in some stupid swamp somewhere has Satan embedded in their brain and they should know better. It's these kinds of people who've rejected the Holy Trinity, (God), believing Satanic garbage that is always available for those sacred children of God that prefer to believe in only what their eyes tell them. That is the express lane to Hell.

4

All About Our
Blessed Mother Mary

I know very well most of you will reject what I have just written. This rejection has been proven over many years considering how the message from our Lord and Savior Jesus Christ was received 2,000 years ago. Surprisingly to me the same thing happened to our Blessed Mother Mary over hundreds of years with her loving apparitions. She told me she appeared 375 times, but we know of only a few. She "laments" about this. People were either scared, disbelieving, or unwilling to tell other people what Mother Mary told them. Let us take her apparition at Fatima. That became a Vatican political football where the Church officials became horrifically political and now Pope Francis just last month as this is written TOLD FALSEHOODS about the third secret. He bold face TOLD a FALSEHOOD that the third sacred has been fulfilled and Russia has been consecrated to the Immaculate Heart of Blessed Mother Mary. NO! Francis is a liar! He made it look like that, but he did not say the proper words as shown in another part of this book.

Another roadblock was the Catholic Church itself. The general attitude of the Church was deep skepticism, disbelief, and outright hiding things from our Father's sacred children. This last action by the Church is what they did to the third secret of Fatima as told by our Blessed Mother Mary. They did so because the third secret was extremely powerful and made the Catholic Church look really bad. As you will see herein, you will read all the contents of the third secret and judge the Church for yourselves.

Without going into a lot of detail, our Heavenly Father through Jesus Christ and Blessed Mother Mary asked me to write a book. One that delivers our Father's message of love, peace, understanding and acceptance to His sacred children on earth. Additionally, Father provided advanced theological information that addresses advanced existential understandings of how all His creation is designed, how it works and where we as Father's sacred children fit into things. Everything in these advanced theological understandings is completely consistent with our Blessed Holy Bible. The title is: God's Grand Design of All Creation for Your Redemption. It begins by answering the question of what exactly are you. The answer is magnificently beautiful.

Remember, each and every one of you is a sacred child of Almighty God. You are a spiritual being living on earth for specific reasons I will not go into now. I have written a booklet titled, "God's Grand Design Booklet I Creation." It is here I have written everything your Heavenly Father wants you to know about your existence. Everything written there is completely consistent with our Christian Biblical literature.

We will start with La Salette, then continue with Garabandal, Lourdes, Zeitoun and finally to Fatima. But first I feel it is very revealing and appropriate I describe what our Blessed Mother Mary's voice sounds like. In a nutshell it is beautiful.

How Does Blessed Mother Mary Speak with Me?

The manner in which Mother Mary's thoughts wind up in a sacred book like this is actually pretty simple. Given our Heavenly Father appointed me as His anointed messenger, which brings with it the ability to speak with the Holy Trinity and our Blessed Mother Mary. Yes, that last sentence is absolutely true but also exceedingly rare.

At the direct request of our holy Almighty Father, I wrote a book that contained what our Father wants all of His sacred children to know. The title is, "God's Grand Design of All Creation for Your Redemption." Now I am writing this book about the End of Times with the help of our Blessed Mother Mary. Blessed Mother Mary has a lot of amazing information for all of God's sacred children.

The Sacred Process

When it is appropriate, I will cloister myself in an incredibly quiet room within my home. I must create the physical conditions necessary so my prayer for all attention centers on our beloved and Blessed

Mother Mary. I have to pray the Our Father and Hail Mary. Additionally, I will pray as much of the rosary as is necessary to completely eliminate any distracting earthly thoughts that may have been bothering me. There are times when I have to conduct spiritual warfare against Satan. He hates me more than you can imagine.

Nonetheless, I am protected. And when I'm peaceful and my attention drifts to our Blessed Mother Mary, I'm ready to ask her questions and I invite her to say what she wants all of God's sacred children to know.

This is such a beautiful and sacred thing to do, preparing to speak with actually not only our Blessed Mother Mary but also our Lord and savior Jesus Christ. Additionally on more rare occasions I will want to ask our loving Heavenly Father a question or two. But what usually happens is I will be engaging in some activity and our Heavenly Father starts talking to me at His will not mine. I remember one time I was away from my computer and our Heavenly Father started to speak with me. I was forced to saying, dear Father, please wait until my speech to text software up and running to make sure everything you say will be preserved for all your sacred children.

While I was preparing the computer and turning on the software, I thought to myself, "good Lord Richard, do you realize what you just did? You actually ask the creator of all that is seen and unseen to wait a minute for you? How awful can you get? But our loving Father waited for the minute or two and then I said, "dear Father I'm ready please tell me anything you wish." And within a fleeting moment that's exactly what He did. I will never forget that moment as long as I live and actually for all the eternity when I am back in the Kingdom.

The Reason Mother Mary Speaks to Me

The reason is so important! I'll tell you how all this came about in my position with the Trinity and Blessed Mother Mary. It is because everything published with regards to our Blessed Mother Mary's apparitions is always secondhand and thirdhand and loaded with opinions that many times are completely misguided and based on only partial information. This does a terrible service to God's sacred children which is YOU!

Additionally, (I will complain about this more later), the Catholic Church has proven a nasty roadblock preventing God's sacred children hearing firsthand and accurately messages our Blessed Mother Mary gave us at her various apparitions. This is especially true with Fatima.

What you hold in your hand has NO INTERFERENCES from the Catholic Church or any other people who wish to manipulate the words of our Blessed Mother Mary. One case in point. Mother Mary asked that the third secret of Fatima be delivered to all of God's sacred children in the year of 1960. That never happened. Why? It is because the third secret does indeed reveal terrible things that will happen to the earth unless mankind repents. But importantly the third secret reveals the vast corruption, apostasy, blasphemy, sexual perversion, and even Satanic worship within the Vatican. Yes, you read that correctly!

I have included other apparitions within this sacred document because of two reasons:

1. Mother Mary asked me to

2. the content of these separations all fit together to produce a picture of the future of God's sacred children on earth. That future is referred to as "The End of Times."

This will all be discussed openly and plainly within this book. Jesus Christ Himself said, "I am the way the truth and the life and no one goes to the Father except by me." Well, the Church has been fighting the release of the truth Blessed Mother Mary has been trying to deliver to God's sacred children for many hundreds of years. The Church has gone so far astray for example as to create a fake Lucia of Fatima so as to drastically water down the true message of Fatima. At least this is what significant evidence shows along with experts that have scientifically proven the lady posing as Lucia today is not the real historical Lucia.

This book contains the authentic words of our Blessed Mother Mary as she wants everyone of God's sacred children to hear firsthand. Many priests, nuns, bishops, and Cardinals have all been sworn to secrecy. So, they have been muffled by the Vatican and other Church powers to prevent you from hearing about what you should know. I HAVE NOT TAKEN ANY OATH OF ANY KIND! So, this book will deliver all of Blessed Mother Mary's messages through her apparitions to God's sacred children, YOU! Fundamentally this means the words of our Blessed Mother Mary are going directly from her to you through the printed words in this book.

She will do this directly. How? It is because your Heavenly Father has asked me to be His Anointed Messenger. As His Anointed Messenger I have been gifted to be able to talk with Blessed Mother Mary directly. Yes! I have been magnificently gifted by our loving Father in Heaven to be able to talk directly with our Blessed Mother Mary and our Lord and savior Jesus Christ. Additionally, our Heavenly Father speaks to me very clearly about assorted items that come up regarding the publication of the books he wants to be written and published for your benefit.

Previous to this book, I have written a small book titled, "God's Grand Design, Booklet I Creation." I suggest you get a copy. Our Father wants you to know what is contained there. Regarding this book, there is no intermediary. Whatever Blessed Mother Mary tells me directly, I transcribe it directly to my computer where a text file is generated. This text file contains the exact words of whatever Blessed Mother Mary tells me.

There are no filters, no priests, bishops, Cardinals, or any other Church related people that will get in the way and pervert and modify and twist the truth of what Blessed Mother Mary has said. She wants everybody to know about the coming times and especially the End of Times which are upon us right now. Since approximately 1960 the world has entered the End of Times. More on that later in this book.

So, what you are about to read is the unfiltered, untwisted, unedited and unmodified words of our Blessed Mother Mary in the messages She's tried to get out to God's sacred children. Therefore, you must realize that this book is sacred from the first page to the last period on the last page. It is sacred truth as said directly by our Blessed Mother Mary, the Mother of God the Mother of our Lord and savior Jesus Christ.

The Beautiful Voice of Mother Mary

I have never seen a description of what Blessed Mother Mary's voice sounds like throughout all my research from many diverse sources that claim to have heard what she says in her apparitions. I don't know why this is because her voice is remarkably distinctive and divine. I have had the beautiful experience of hearing her melodious language many times during the course of writing this book. Imagine a loving human based Heavenly Angelic female voice in your mind, you would be describing Blessed Mother Mary in her fullness of love and gentleness for each and every one of God's sacred children.

I can describe her voice as ever so feminine and gentle speaking slowly and softly while caressing a sincere love that projects a magnificent divine quality to what she says. Her voice with its softness and its ever so caring tone of love really does gently sooth my mind and it makes me feel so wonderfully loved.

Her divine love for me feels like it is contained in every word she says. When she speaks of warnings to all of God's sacred children like the third secret of Fatima, there is a tone of urgency and deep concern in her voice. One beautiful characteristic of how Blessed Mother speaks is that when she wants to emphasize a word, she's stretches out the word more than the others. For example, if she wants to say, "that is a real problem," it will sound like she is stretching out that phrase a little longer than normal. Poetically speaking her voice is like a soft breeze rustling through the trees with a love that defies description. Her loving and lilting voice is like a divine touch to my soul. Oh, how I wish each of you could hear with your own ears our Blessed Mother Mary. But, one day you will after you enter the paradise, we call the Heavenly Kingdom.

She is never at a loss for words and when she explains something she also includes related thoughts that amplify what she means. She knows me ever so well. There have been times, actually many times, when I suffer from my chronic migraine headaches and am in a lot of pain when I want to speak with her. She knows how I feel and many times she suggests we delay our conversation and I need to have rest for a time. I take my strong pain medicine and after a while I feel better, and Mother Mary knows that and then we continue what we intended to begin with.

There have been times also when I have been very tired many times from headache pain and even though the pain is gone, I'm just exhausted and even Mother Mary knows this too. And even then, she suggests I rest. She has told me to rest many times because our Lord and Savior Jesus Christ told her I work too hard especially when I was sick for two months early in the year 2024.

Mother Mary, The Link Between Earth and Heaven

Most people believe Mother Mary is the Mother of Jesus Christ and was raised up to Heaven by God. Some people know she has had apparitions that are miraculous. Beyond that, people do not know much. The fact is Mother Mary is extremely active in her sacred attempts to bring redemption to all of God sacred children. You will be amazed at everything she has done and is currently doing to bring about a Heavenly future for as many of God's sacred children on earth as she possibly can.

I bring you the below information because its message is twofold and enormously powerful. Most Christians think of our Blessed Mother Mary as the Mother of God and who appears on occasion in apparitions with children emphasizing the need for prayer, sacrifice, penance and praying the rosary. Our Mother Mary plays an active role in helping those of goodwill to avoid catastrophes on earth.

Her importance goes far deeper than just that if that isn't enough. Our Blessed Mother Mary also maintains holy friendships and communications with people who were still on earth. The below story about Pope John II talking with her and abiding by what she asks Him to do. This is so powerful and goes way beyond apparitions. Remember please, it is our Blessed Mother Mary that will put an end to Satan by virtue of her magnificent love and her Immaculate Heart! It is our Blessed Mother Mary's Immaculate Heart that will crush the head of Satan. How? It is by her Immaculate intense love.

I am fortunate enough to be one of the people our Blessed Mother Mary wishes to talk to. In my case it is for writing the books that contain the messages of our holy Father in Heaven, our Lord and

Savior Jesus Christ and of course our Blessed Mother Mary. This book is completely dedicated to our Blessed Mother Mary.

March 14, 2024
Spoken by our Almighty Father's Anointed Messenger

My dear sacred child of God, this book you hold in your hands is a Sacred Document. It is so because it contains the direct words of our Blessed Mother Mary. All sacred words contained within will always be presented in bold and italicized print. My words as author and Anointed Messenger of our Heavenly Father will always be in regular Times New Roman text. Why is it this way? It is because Blessed Mother Mary is far more important than me God's Anointed Messenger.

Here is the first of many things Mother Mary will say within this Book.

April 17, 2024
Our Beloved Blessed Mother Mary:

My dearest son Richard, you have worked so extremely hard to bring the truth of our Holy Father to His sacred children on earth. You are so very correct that our Father's sacred children have now entered into The End of Times. As you have observed, dearest son. That falling away from the love and the rules of life that our Father has put forth for the benefit and the happiness of His children on earth has been under increasing attack by Satan. As you have said, you have observed the crumbling away of God's manner of living on earth so as to return to Him in the Heavenly Kingdom for all eternity.

Especially dear son, your book titled God's Grand Design of All Creation for Your Redemption, is a magnificent piece of Biblical literature that you have written in common everyday language so everybody can understand. It is slowly gaining in popularity and will continue as such. I am honored dear son, dear Anointed Messenger of our Father, to be with you writing about my apparitions throughout the many years until now.

One thing I want your readers to know is that in your research you have found that there have been about thirty-four apparitions of me, mostly to little children. I have chosen little children because they have not been in the world long enough to become jaded, and their minds are still fresh, close to their Heavenly Father and honest. But in some cases, as you have found out like La Salette in France, the children became afraid due to the elders that surrounded them. Maximin could not stand the pressure and revoked saying that he told a falsehood. He did not. Both you and I know this.

Another thing that people do not realize is that I have appeared to many others since my son was on the earth. In actual fact, my dear son, I have appeared many times more than the 34 apparitions that have been published to be read by God's sacred children in the Church. Most of the time the children that I appeared to after a time became exceedingly frightened and did not tell anyone of what occurred. My message to everyone is always ever so simple. It is basically love, peace, penance, sacrifice and to always say the Holy Rosary.

People continue to not understand the Almighty power of what I have just mentioned. Why is this so? It is because doing these things strengthens enormously people's love and connection directly to the Trinity and me. This strong connection destroys Satan's ability to cause agony, pain, suffering in the world. Basically, the closer you are to your Heavenly Father, the farther away Satan becomes. Satan's violence and destructive temptations do not stand a chance against prayer, sacrifice, penance, and the Holy Rosary.

This is why in doing these things great spiritual power comes to all those who listen to what I have to say. With this spiritual power across many people in the world, ever so many wars in the world would be avoided.

However, the time of Satan is at hand. To you my dearest Anointed Messenger of our Holy Father, what you have said is that the world has now entered into the preliminary stages of the end of times. You have also stated that you know Satan is working within the Vatican and yes, my dear son Pope France is under the control of Satan and is the last pope. Frightening as this may be, things will get worse before they get better. In another part of this book you are writing, I will expand upon my prophecies all of which will come true before my son returns to earth.

A horrific number of lives and souls will be lost in the coming years. Dear son, I suggest you at this time document all the wars in the world right now. It is Heartbreaking yet I knew all of this would happen and so now you too.

Let us, you, and I, now proceed with far more details in this magnificent Book and I want you to center upon my apparitions that talk about the End of Times.

I love you ever so much my dearest son. You are protected and always in my prayers.

Your Blessed Mother Mary

Question: Dear Mother Mary, if you don't mind being quantitative as I am. Could you put a numerical figure on just how many times you appeared to different children in separate places on earth to deliver your messages and your warnings?

Answer: *Oh, of course dear son, I will. You may be surprised but remember I also appeared without saying anything to anybody. It is my image of love and peace that appears to people to remind them of not only me but my messages of love, peace, sacrifice, prayer, the mass, and the powerful Rosary. These are too numerous to mention because ever so many thousands of people see my image but then my effect on their prayer life slowly fades away.*

But regarding the times in which I have spoken to selected ones of God's sacred children. And have not been reported the number you are looking for is 375 times that I have spoken to the sacred children of God. My appearance almost always produces fear among the children. Many times, they do not report what they saw because of their fear of getting into trouble with the elders. Other times elders ignore what they say thinking they are just making up fanciful stories. Even when the children describe my appearances. To the parents and local elders all along with in the contents of what I have said, the event gets tangled up and confused by people in the Church.

Many times, even the local priests and bishops accused the children of lying and this is what happened at La Salette. They reported what they saw and what was said. One of the children disappeared from the scene and the other, Maximin simply denied our encounter and said he told a falsehood. However, there are particularly important and shining examples of when things mostly go right and the legitimate appearance of mine reaches the higher authorities in the Church. But even then, due to the honest content like in Fatima, the Church hierarchy decides to hide my words of prophecy because they think it makes the Church look bad. Lastly, Garabandal, Akita and Medjugorje are good examples of things going properly and I would like you to emphasize these in this magnificent book you are writing.

People, God's sacred children must know what is coming and that things have already started that are part of the End of Times. This is not the end of the world; it is the End of Times which will be horrifically painful in so many ways that I will tell you later in this terrific book.

Mother Mary's Loving Thoughts to Me Your Author

Today, Sunday, February 18, 2024, when I woke, Mother Mary was immediately on my mind. Even though I was praying the Our Father as I always do first thing in the morning as my feet hit the floor but still sitting on the edge of the bed. It was intuitively obvious to me our Blessed Mother wanted to tell me important things that are on her mind and I can do my research later. Our Blessed Mother wanted me to do today exactly what I am now doing, which is to document what she wants to tell all of God's sacred children. This will be published in the second book with the title," *God's Grand Design, Blessed Mother Mary Speaks Her Apparitions and The End of Times*."

I perceive an intense sense of urgency in creating this book. And so, it will be I will devote 100% of my efforts in fulfilling anything and everything our Blessed Mother wants me to say and to do.

As a reminder, our Blessed Mother's words will be transcribed directly from what she tells me from the spiritual realm. And I will repeat word for word what she says to me in the computer software I have that is speech to text. In this manner 100% of everything you read within this booklet are Mother Mary's direct words.

5

The Catholic Church Is No Longer What You Think It Is

I am heartbroken to have had to write these truths about our beloved Catholic Church, specifically the Vatican, NOT our local parishes. The rest of this book is dedicated to the absolute truth of the Catholic Church and the way it exists on earth today. When I was a little boy, I went to Saint Tarcisius elementary school in Chicago IL. It was run by a bunch of German nuns back in the early 1950's right after World War 2. These German nuns were just plain cruel to us kids. They wore huge black garments with a black hood on their head and large rosary beads around their waist. And every time they would walk down the hall they would click and clack all the way. They could never sneak up on us kids as we all could hear them coming.

In each classroom there were between 60 and 70 of us kids all of which were the firstborn of our armed forces that beat the hell out of the German army. So, it is not surprising these women were seeking revenge against the kids of our armed forces that won World War 2 and completely destroyed Germany, their homeland. They basically taught us to hate religion, Especially Catholicism. However, over the years when it came time for my little kids to go to school, I chose a Catholic education for them. All the way from first grade through graduation at Santa Clara University, a Jesuit school.

Why would I do that? Because I went through the public school system, and it stunk with all sorts of bullies and other BS going on no matter where you looked. Also, the Catholic education system changed greatly in the intervening years and the Catholic sisters we're far nicer and very constructive and caring about the kids. My kids all got taught fundamental Christianity and Catholicism which is an incredibly good thing.

However, that is no longer the case in the Catholic Church or Catholic schools. Additionally, there have been awful infiltration of Satan into the Vatican, and I will get into that in this next section I never thought I would write. But what I'm going to tell you as painful as it is, it is completely true, and it has to do with the End of Times. Everyone already knows about the sexual predator priests and the cover-ups by the Vatican. Actually, that is part of the End of Times prophecies. What I'm going to talk about is far different than that and in many ways worse.

And the remaining part of this book we will go through how Satan has infiltrated the Vatican and as a result has gravely affected all Vatican activities which I will show you with pictures. This will serve as a foundational essay for us to examine Mother Mary's apparitions, her all-important apparitions at Fatima Portugal in 1917. You will see our Satanically infiltrated Vatican and doing everything to hide the truth. The truth of what Blessed Mother Mary said at Fatima Portugal regarding the End of Times which we are already living in. The End of Times started in the early 1960s with the presidency of Lyndon Baines Johnson, one of the most crooked and dishonest human beings ever to walk the face of the earth.

The Fake Consecration of Russia To The Immaculate Heart of Blessed Mother Mary

The very first and most important item regarding the third secret of Fatima is Blessed Mother Mary's request to have Russia properly consecrated to the Immaculate Heart of our Blessed Mother Mary. As of the date this is written May 29, 2024, Russia has yet to be consecrated to the Immaculate Heart of Blessed Mother Mary. Pope Francis said he did it.

NO! POPE FRANCIS IS A LIAR!

Pope Francis pretended to perform the consecration with the words he used were completely wrong on purpose. This is what he should have said. He is the Pope. He knows full well what the proper words are to say. But not only did he purposely choose NOT to say those words but doing so would have prevented the on-going war between Russia and Ukraine. Millions of innocent people have been killed because of Pope Francis. Get the connection yet? For me, your humble Anointed Messenger of our Heavenly Father, it seems Pope Francis wanted this war. What other explanation is there? If he only said these words, there would have been no war.

Additionally, Pope Francis lied big time by declaring that there is no third secret of Fatima! A major portion of the remaining parts of this book presents the "exact words of our Blessed Mother Mary in great detail all about the third secret Pope Francis now says does not exist!"

Question: What was it Pope John II was exactly supposed to say when he had the opportunity to consecrate Russia to your Immaculate Heart in 1962?

Answer: *It was really only one sentence among the many that he said during the mass that he celebrated. Instead of just referring to "and all others" which very indirectly includes Russia, he should have said in very plain terms,*

"I Also Consecrate Russia To The Immaculate Heart of Our Blessed Mother Mary."

It would have been that simple my dear son but yes, he was under a lot of pressure not to do so from people who were ill-willed due to political reasons.

Question: On another note, dear Mother Mary, I read one article recently that indicated Pope Francis will read the third secret of Fatima and consecrate Russia to your Immaculate Heart. I don't want to be a cynic, but I do not personally believe any of this will happen. I would love to hear what it is you want the world to know regarding your comments.

Answer: *Almighty dear son, Jesus was right when he told me your questions can be very penetrating, direct and to the point. Thank you for that. Pope Francis will not read the third secret of Fatima. Because,* *as you my son already know, it makes the Church not only look bad but also it reveals the sinister forces that are already in the Vatican. I believe that is the last thing he would ever contemplate doing.*

The chances are not good that Pope Francis will consecrate Russia to my Sacred Heart. That will set into motion the wonderful expansion of Christian beliefs within the Russian people. However, because this declaration has come so late it will not be in a strong enough force to avoid the coming wars regarding Russia and others against the Western Christian world. <u>Had Pope John II said the consecration for Russia, we would not have the warlike situation we have today.</u>

In general, people to this day do not at all understand the loving significance of our Blessed Mother Mary's Immaculate Heart. This second secret refers directly to the devotion to the Immaculate Heart of our Blessed Mother Mary. Consecration to the Immaculate Heart of Mother Mary has the power to alter History and prevent future wars.

Note: The Immaculate heart of our Blessed Mother Mary is no fairy tale! It has real and vast power behind it for the good of all of God's sacred children on earth. For example, Jorge had cardinal Bergoglio Delivered the one powerful sentence to consecrate Russia to the Immaculate heart of our Blessed Mother Mary, Russia would not have invaded Ukraine. Countless hundreds of thousands of innocent people would be alive today conducting their personal productive lives. Pope Francis did not do that and is lying when he said he did. Pope Francis has blood on his hands

Question: I am wondering what is the blessing or how once for example Russia is consecrated to your Immaculate heart, spiritually speaking how does that directly affect God's sacred children living in Russia? I envision something like a cloud of Heavenly grace will descend upon the people within Russia. And that will result in them turning away from whatever is bad and turning them toward Biblical teachings and behaving according to the three summary rules I published in my previous book. Am I anywhere close to how your Immaculate heart spreads to the people?

Answer: *Wow, my dear son! That is a monumentally detailed question, and it shows your insatiable thirst for Godly knowledge. Additionally, the manner and which you surmised the mechanism of my Immaculate heart is remarkably close to what actually happens in real life.*

If Pope Francis actually uttered the sentence that you have put in this book twice, that would release a huge number of Heavenly Blessings. Godly Blessings that pour out from our Heavenly Father and into the people that the consecration is meant for. It is enormous holy energy that comes from Heaven and enters into the spiritual hearts of the people. This is even true for those who are disbelievers and high up in the political structure of a particular country. For example, if that criminal Pope Francis did what he said he did, that would trigger the release of monumental proportion of loving energy into the hearts of the communist leaders of Russia. Including Vladimir Putin himself along with everyone in government everyone in the army and so forth. All of these people would start to question what the heck are we doing? They would start to seriously question what they have done and what they are doing to destroy God's sacred children. Many of them would respond and they would leave the battlefield and go home.

Satan would be defeated resoundingly. The same thing would occur on Ukraine side of the war equation. But <u>my dear son as you know it is Satan that controls Pope Francis</u>. It is the command from Satan to the Pope "do not declare the consecration of Russia and the Ukraine to my Sacred Heart" because Satan knows that would end the war. And Satan wants to destroy every single one of God's sacred children so the war must go on. And the Pope has the power to stop it, but he refused. He faked the consecration and then told falsehoods about it.

Question: Are there any other people on this planet that has the power to bestow and consecrate the Pope to your Immaculate heart? Why do we have to be limited by this Satanic Pope? Let's just bypass him since many people think he is really not the Pope due to his falsehoods regarding his internal beliefs of Christianity as your Son and my savior Jesus Christ established it. I know you know what I am thinking.

Answer: *Wow, my dearest of sons! I again am amazed and your dedication for the world and the love of all mighty God and his creations. I wish I could say it is all that easy but to consecrate a country or someone the person doing that must have position power within the physical realm. <u>In the case of consecrating Russia, one has to be in the Direct Line of popes that traces back to Saint Peter when my son canonized him as the first Pope</u>.*

Comment: Well, I figured the restriction might be something just like what you said. When I was in Civil Air Patrol an auxiliary of the United States Air Force, rank was everything. It did not matter how competent or good the person was if he had the appropriate rank that's all that is needed.

I had this theoretical thought cross my mind. What if the power of consecration could be given to priests. They could consecrate everybody, and the holy power of love would descend down and into the hearts of people. What a wonderful way to eliminate sin. Yes, dear Blessed Mother, I know this is fanciful, but it was just a thought.

Response: *Although your thought may be fanciful it is an absolutely beautiful thought and I thank you for that*.

Question: Most Christians view prayers as a religious duty that has some unknown but positive effect on what they're praying about. Prayers could be about almost anything and are ALWAYS very welcome by not only the Holy Trinity but also our Blessed Mother Mary. Above we came to understand the enormous power of the consecration to Mother Mary's Immaculate Heart. With this being said, I would like to explore the power and positive effects on our Father's sacred children in their lives. Is this out of bounds dear Mother?

Answer: *Oh, my dearest son I just love the intensity, dedication, and love that you show others of God's sacred children on earth. This is a question that I know many devout Catholics and Christians have in the back of their minds. So, with that I very much love to answer this.*

Using the example of consecrating Russia to my Immaculate heart generally speaking the same thing happens on a personal prayer basis but at a reduced level. This is because, instead of having many millions of people being the recipients of God's loving energy that will flow into their hearts as sacred graces come. The same thing really does happen when a person prays. There is never, I want to emphasize this there is never a case where prayers go unheard. As you have written in your previous book titled God's grand design of all creation for your redemption. It is impossible for the Trinity not to hear the slightest prayer or the biggest prayer from anyone of your Father's sacred children. As you outlined and your previous book, God so loves each of his children that he left part of himself within each of his sacred children. When each of them was created within the heavenly Kingdom many billions of years ago.

Your heavenly Father always knows exactly what is best for each sacred child and when a prayer is said, it will certainly be answered 100% of the time. But since your Father can see across all aspects of time, he will tune his response so that the most benefit will be given to each separate child.

This is different than consecrating an entire country. Because there are so many different people that personalizing responses is something that will not work but certainly works on an individual basis when individual prayers are being said to the Trinity. Also, when prayers with the heart that is true to Almighty God, that certainly strengthens the relationship between our heavenly Father and the sacred child that said the prayer.

As you said above, all prayers are real and powerful. Thank you for asking this wonderful question that does indeed impact every one of your Father's sacred children.

I love you my dear child.

The Aftermath of The Popes Refusal to Release the Third Fatima Secret and Not Consecrate Russia

The spiritual punishments apparently started shortly after 1960 because of the holy Father s refusal to release Fatima's third secret and to consecrate Russia to the Immaculate Heart of our Blessed Mother Mary. (Authors note: just how stupid can a Pope be? Unless he has a hidden agenda)

1. Father Malachi Martin said "many cardinals, bishops and priests are falling like leaves into hell.

2. Faith disappears in several countries and continents.

3. Many of the elect will lose their faith.

4. Things will get so bad that if our Lady does not intervene no one will be saved.

5. God will withdraw His grace.

6. Father Malachi told Art Bishop that apostasy in the Church was the background or context of the third secret.

7. if our Lady's orders are not obeyed spiritual punishment would result.

8. God withdrawing His grace is a painful thing for Him, because it is like sabotaging His own sacred will that, "all men be saved and come to the full knowledge of the truth."

9. Satan will now gain power in the upper echelons of the Church; Satan wants to gain power even in the highest echelons of the Church.

10. the last Pope will be under the control of Satan. Now Pope Francis is the 112th Pope which has been prophesies to be the last Pope. Additionally, when you examine our Pope's goals in the Vatican it fundamentally is toward creating a secularized Catholic faith. More on that later.

11. Father Malachi Martin agreed the last Pope will be under the control of Satan.

12. Tribulations will follow.

There is a prophecy Satan can invade the Citadel or also known as the Vatican. They will have power for one thousand years. Then our bill asked, "how close are they/" Malachi Martin responded, "very close, frighteningly close."

Then Art Bell asked, "how will we know and how will you know when Satan takes over and the 1000 years begins?"

We will know this by a series of facts which amount to the following: [1]

1. The basic tenants, beliefs of Christianity will be played down to zero.

2. And will matter no longer in normal society and nations.

3. For those who are supposed to be the custodians and supposed to be the administrators of the word and distributors of His grace have stopped all that.

4. It will talk down to secular terms and rather overnight as far as I can see.

5. Then it will suddenly dawn on people that, hey this St. has gone completely awry.

6. The Third Secret provides for "a punishment of a spiritual nature." "Apostasy in the Church forms the background or context of the Third Secret. Apostasy now begins. But the punishment envisaged for the Secret is very real, physical punishment is, and they are terrible!" "Just kill a billion people"

---

[1] The Decline and Fall of The Roman Church, Fr. Malichi Martin

This was the exchange between Father Malachi Martin and Art Bell.

Also, according to this website, which I recommend titled "return to tradition.org" it used to be the Church in working with governments. There would be cooperation where the governments would try to back up the morality of Christianity in secular society by their governance. This is no longer the case, and it can be horrifically demonstrated in the United States of America through the Democrat party and their anti-Christian policies. More on this in another section of this book.

Malachi Martin speaks at an event called "Paranormal Continuum":

1. Everything is becoming integrated today, morals, and ethics today of individual communities and groups and ethics have become completely degraded into materialistic secular terms and hedonistic aims.

2. That is the reign of evil. In directly contravention to the will of God who is the sovereign master and creator of all things.

3. Evil is more organized, more integrated worldwide which comes out as the deification of man,

Evidence of this secular perversion includes:

1. The expansion of the sacraments to give access to the sacraments to those who are unrepentant sinners without calling them to conversion.

2. Blessings of James Martin type and those in irregular situations that contravene Church law.

3. The open debate on changing the Churches morality and teachings on moral issues, all of it is happening within this backdrop.

4. These are some of the clearest signs of the Church increasingly under the influence of Satan.

5. The mockery of the faith being conducted in sports stadiums.

6.   Also, Catholics in the Western world are not caring or agreeing with the liberalization and progressiveness that is being developed within the Catholic Church.

7.   Heresies pushed by Rome, now most Catholics just shrug.

Mother Mary stated WW I would end, followed by another world war during the reign of Pope Pius XI (Pope till 1939). The world situation was rapidly crumbling toward war during the reign of Pope Pius XI. WWII began in September 1939. This second war would come if people continued offending our Heavenly Father and if Russia is not consecrated and does not convert to Christianity. Remember our Blessed Mother Mary said this in 1917. This second secret specifically requests Russia be consecrated to the Immaculate Heart of Mary.

Pope Francis was on elected March 13, 2013, but he did not consecrate Russia and Ukraine to the Immaculate Heart of Blessed Mother Mary. That was nine years into His pontificate. Sadly, on February 24, 2022, Russia invaded Ukraine. This invasion is seen as an escalation of the Russo-Ukrainian war that started in 2014. [2]

As a Catholic Christian, I cannot help wondering if this war that has taken hundreds of thousands of lives would not have happened if Pope Francis acted years earlier as our Blessed Mother Mary asked.

---

[2] Dates from Wikipedia

6

The Anti-Christ Is Now in The Vatican.

The Catholic Church Is Turning Against Its Own Teachings. [3]

Here is just one manifestation of the prophecies of our Blessed Mother Mary. Back in 1917 at Fatima exactly what you are reading now is what was prophesized an exceptionally long time ago. Cardinal Sarah (shown Here) has been accusing the Catholic Church and its leadership of being complicit towards fluid and practical atheism within the Church.[4]

---

[3]https://Catholicherald.co.uk/cardinal-sarah-denounces-atheistic-western-bishops-who-prefer-the-world-to-the-cross/

[4] Joe McLean, A Catholic Take – A Radio Program

We pretend to be Catholics but in fact we behave and believe as pagans and unbelievers. He has denounced western atheistic bishops and leaders that prefer the world over the cross.

Women priests, deaconesses, homosexuality, same-gender marriages are now becoming increasingly rampant within the Church our Lord and savior Jesus Christ founded. The occurrence of these kinds of disgusting events has indeed been prophesized by more than just our Blessed Mother Mary. This is something that was told about in 1917 during one of her six apparitions in Fatima Portugal.

During the week of April 20th, 2024, a German Bishop ordained thirteen deaconesses. He made a big deal about this and even passed out certificates of some kind to make it all with its pomp and circumstance feel like a real ordination. Personally, I am certain these new deaconesses are certainly not. Makes everybody feel good that believes in apostasy, but these women are not legitimate in any way shape or form. Call this blasphemy or apostasy or any other anti-Church label and it is happening in openness within the Catholic Church. The German Catholic Church is also in favor of women priests and homosexuality. Cardinal Parolin says all the blasphemous changes Pope Francis wants to make within the Church must be permanent where there is no possibility of it being rescinded, no reversals or reforms. Father Malachi Martin has said the identical thing and has added that there are even Satanic rituals being performed within the Vatican. Before you reject this thought, all of this has been foretold by our Blessed Mother Mary during her apparitions at Fatima.

I will reveal no names for their protection. But think about that for a while and put yourself in the shoes of an honest priest in the Priestly community. Just how hard must it be to live with the priests that have sex with teenage children and with other priests within the Church. How can they possibly keep their mouth shut. Because if they open their mouths and reveal the Satanist activities within the Catholic Church, they will have no support for their lives like food shelter and clothing.

'The former prefect of the Vatican's Congregation for Divine Worship and the Sacraments said so many bishops desired to be 'loved by the world'. That they have forgotten that Christianity calls them to be "signs of contradiction."

The 78-year-old cardinal also repeated His criticism of Fiducia Supplicans, the Vatican document that provides for the blessings of couples involved in same-sex unions. Insisting that it is not just traditional African culture but Catholic teaching itself which makes the document unacceptable.' "Many Western prelates are tetanized [paralyzed] by the idea of opposing the world," the cardinal said. "They dream of being loved by the world; they've lost the desire to be a sign of contradiction." [5]

Father Malachi Martin said "many cardinals, bishops and priests are falling like leaves into hell. He went on to say Satan is not already inside the Vatican but exerts heavy influence as well. [6] The Father should know very well what goes on in the Vatican.

---

[5] Cardinal Sarah denounces 'atheistic' Western bishops who prefer the world to the cross - Catholic Herald

[6] Malachi Martin: The Enthronement of Lucifer in The Vatican (youtube.com)

Evidence Pope Francis is obsessed with Satan has become more obvious in recent times. Even liberal news outlet CNN has noticed his fascination with Satan. There is particularly good reason for his interest you will be shocked by later on in this book.

CNN [7]

Pope Francis seems to be obsessed with the devil.

His tweets and homilies about Satan, the Accuser, the Evil One, the Father of lies, the Ancient Serpent, the Tempter, the Seducer, the Great Dragon, the Enemy and just plain "demon" are now legion.

For Francis, the devil is not a myth, but a real person. Many modern people may greet the Pope's insistence on the devil with a dismissive, cultural affectation, indifference, or at the most indulgent curiosity.

Yet Francis refers to the devil continually. He does not believe him to be a myth, but a real person, the most insidious enemy of the Church. Several of my theologian colleagues have said he has gone a bit overboard with the devil and hell! We may be tempted to ask, why in the devil is Pope Francis so involved with the prince of demons?

Malachi Martin: End Of Times - The Enthronement of Lucifer in The Vatican [8] Father Malachi Martin authored a book called Windswept House. Published in 1996 three years before Father martin passed away. This book is labeled "Faction" why? Because however it does contain actual information regarding the End of Times and the actions of Satan in this world. He sprinkles some fictional information in this book like the dates of something or somebody's name and so on. Please realize Father Martins sole purpose in authoring his book is to describe what the third secret of Fatima says. Father Martin does not have the supreme advantage I do in that I can just ask Mother Mary.

---

[7] Why is Pope Francis so obsessed with the devil? | CNN

Which I certainly will later on time wise when I gather my thoughts on what I should ask her about this horrific enthronement of Lucifer inside the Vatican.

Remember, this event was prophesized many hundreds of years earlier by multiple people. This book is an exceptionally good chronicle of the Satanic events that took place inside the Vatican. This is the way Father Martin chose to circumvent the ironclad oath he was forced to take regarding the third secret of Fatima. He embedded facts about what was said from our Blessed Mother Mary at Fatima into various parts of the fictional novel he wrote. This man was no dummy.

"In an interview, Father Martin said the following text from the book listed above is factual based on actual events. "Whosoever shall, by means of this inner Chapel, be designated and chosen as the final in the line successor in the petrine office. And shall by His very oath of office commit himself. And all he does command to be the willing instrument and collaborator with the builders of man's home on earth and throughout man's cosmos. He shall transform the ancient enmity into friendship, tolerance, and assimilation as these are a falsehood to the models of birth, education, work, finance, commerce, industry, learning, culture, living and giving life, dying and death. *So shall the coming age of man be modeled*."

The above oath centers only on man and earth. God is nowhere in the picture. This is what you would expect from Satan Himself and creating disastrous nice sounding words. I will also tell you this as a secondary thought. Every word that is pledged above is Satanic and also is used frequently by the Democrat party in the United States of America. If you are a Democrat, you are not a Christian rather you are following the precepts of this Satanic pledge.

Also look at the above vocabulary and terms like man's cosmos. That is diametrically opposed to all Biblical literature. I could go on, but I would end up writing an encyclopedia. Also please notice these nicety nice words are used by Pope Francis today. He does not use Apostolic terminology and thoughts. Back to the issue at hand which is Satan inside the Vatican. Father Brian Harrison knew Father Malachi Martin. Father Harrison said the following:

"I can clarify what Father Martin said was the true date of the Luciferian enthronement inside the Vatican with the following information from 1/4 century ago I have never made public until now. In the last decade of Malachi Martins life, I became a personal friend of His and would visit Him in His Manhattan apartment whenever I was in New York. In the section headed "1963" in the prologue of <u>Windswept House</u>, we read this shocking ceremony enthroned "the fallen Angel Lucifer" in the Chapel of Saint Paul took place on June 29, 1963. That being the feast of Saints Peter and Paul, the eve of the coronation of the newly elevated Pope Paul VI."

It is celebrated gloatingly the long prepared for arrival of a Pope more open to modernist changes than any of His predecessors. Around the time the book was published in 1996, Father Martin told me that this date was indeed factional. (Meaning it is Historically correct), and that the true date of this blasphemous act of devilry, coordinated with a corresponding ceremony on the American side of the Atlantic, come was actually one day later. That is, it took place the night after Saint Paul's VI coronation in Saint Peters square on the afternoon of Sunday, June 30. Malachi told me it was indeed carried out in the Chapel of Saint Paul, as the book windswept house says, and it began at midnight on the night of June 30 / July 1, 1963.

"Father Malachi Martin goes on to say the following. "Pope John Paul II came up against the irremovable presence of a malign strength in His own Vatican and in certain bishops' chanceries. It is what knowledgeable Churchmen call the 'super force." Rumors are always difficult to verify, tide its installation to the beginning of Pope Paul VI's reign in 1963. Indeed, Paul alluded somberly to the "the smoke of

Satan which has entered the sanctuary" and oblique reference to an enthronement ceremony by (the followers of the devil) inside the Vatican." [9]

Father Martin certainly is not the only high-ranking priest within the Catholic Church to resist the onslaught of Satan. The late exorcist Father Amorth provided keen insight into the status of Satan within the Vatican. The following is an excerpt from an interview with Father Amorth: [10]

Question: Father, you write of dialogues you have had with Satan. Have you ever seen Him?

Answer: He responded by saying, Satan is pure spirit. He often appears as something else to mislead. He appeared to Padre Pio as Jesus, to frighten Him. He sometimes appears as a raging animal...

Question: You have said publicly you believe, referring to the current Church scandals, Satan is in the Vatican. Do you still believe this?"

Answer: Today Satan rules the world. The masses no longer believe in God. And yes, Satan is in the Vatican.

Pope Francis, A Modern Day Satanic Theological Tyrant [11]
April 26th, 2024

Everything you will read in the next couple of pages is from CNA, the Catholic News Agency on April 26th, 2024.

Tyrants and dishonest politicians always start out their quest for conquering a people by using really good sounding language that is

---

[9] https://www.youtube.com/watch?v=MD2XKN4wRKk

[10] https://www.youtube.com/watch?v=MD2XKN4wRKk

[11] https://www.Catholicnewsagency.com/news/255887/pope-francis-calls-for-paradigm-shift-in-theology-for-world-of-today

ambiguous enough to where people hear what it is they want to hear. Dictators love to appear as if they are bringing high-class thought processes to the masses. Such that will solve all their problems and as the worst president in U.S. History Barack Obama said we must bring, change, and change for the sake of change." We must bring equity. If you work half as hard you still get full pay. Remember equity means equal outcome, not equal opportunity.

Does anybody really know what that meant? No. But what that brought was horrific racial separations and hatred between the races and phrases like white supremacy was born out of that nice sounding word change. The term white supremacy is a horrific and Satanic way of pitting one group of God's sacred children against another group. In other words, it fosters hatred which is exactly a characteristic of Satan Himself and all of His followers.

The word equity sounds good. But what it means is that no matter whether you try hard and work hard or not in school you will get the same grade as everyone else. If you are naturally good in math let's, say, the Democrats will say you got that talent unfairly, so all other students must be graded easier than you to make up the different. Democrats goal is EVERYBODY MUST BE IDENTICAL NO MATTER HOW HARD THEY WORK OR NOW! This is exactly the Communist manifesto. Hard work or effort is no longer rewarded. In school the lunkhead sitting next to you sitting on his fingers will get the same grade you got. Equity means equal result not equal opportunity. Work very hard but get the same as someone who did not. Ideas like this destroy cultures and nations.

God granted each separate sacred child a unique set of talents to be used while on earth. Everyone IS different. Equality and equity are designed to destroy our Heavenly Father's plan for us.

Question: Dear Blessed Mother Mary, is there anything else you feel necessary to add?

Answer: *Yes, I do dear son. Satan is nefarious in his plan for destroying your Father s sacred children. The disgusting Democrat plan being to make everyone the same brings unseen horrors with it.*

For those children in school that do not apply themselves, are lazy and do not try to learn their school lessons. They will get the idea that society owes them just because they are who they are. They will think that they are entitled to anything they want just because they want it. Gone is the linkage between effort and reward. This breads resentment and hatred.

For those who do work hard only to see their efforts taken away from themselves will stop working hard and this brings down the living standards in a culture or society. So, you end up with less goods and services with a load of people who feel entitled to all that without working for it.

This can only be a breeding ground for chaos, hatred, confusion, and people at each other's throats. Our country will be like Cuba where everybody shares starvation equally. This Democrat plan is pure Satan my dear son.

Pope Francis Wants to Destroy the Church and Catholicism.

Remember my dear sacred children of God come, cardinal Bergoglio came from Argentina a very socialist / communist country. Pope Francis is doing pretty much the same damn thing. On Thursday April 11, 2024, the Catholic News agency reported this headline: Pope Francis calls for a" paradigm shift" in the apology for the world of today". Does anybody care to take a guess at what that means? What Hitler and Mussolini said right before World War II sounded really good to the people. What they got was enormous amounts of death and destruction. I put Pope Francis in the same category.

President Barack Obama did the same thing running for president. His slogan was, "hope and change." What we got instead was identity politics and hateful rhetoric like white people are evil because they have "white privilege." Never mind that white privilege does not exist. If you disbelieve me go out on the streets and ask random people what is the definition of white privilege? They will not know the answer and we will fumble around trying to think of something. It is this type of situation that is born right out of Satan's playbook.

One other thing dear sacred child of God, <u>our Blessed Mother Mary herself told me personally Pope Francis is indeed the Anti-Christ</u>. I repeat, **<u>Pope Francis is the Anti-Christ</u>**. He is under control of Satan. [12]

Pope Francis Wants to Combine Our Beloved Catholic Church with Many Other Religions Such as Islam, Buddhism etc.

Pope Francis wants to destroy our Beloved Church by combining it with all the other religions in the world. In this manner he will make our Church disappear into the fog of so many conflicting religious doctrines. Satan is clever and this is the best way to achieve pure evil.

This is how he is attempting to do it.

1. To do this he calls for 'paradigm shift' in Catholic theology for the world of today. He will use ambiguous fancy words like paradigm to hide the true meanings and his intentions. [13]

2. Pope Francis is calling for a paradigm shift. Where Catholic theology takes a much broader view, a widespread view, of engagement with the world that includes contemporary science, modern culture throughout the earth, and people's lived experiences. (I bet you do not know the definition of these words that will end up controlling your life)

3. A new document titled Ad Theologian Comes from the Pontifical Academy of Theology. This "theology can only develop in a culture of dialogue and encounter between different traditions and different knowledge, between

---

[12] Antipope Francis' Notable Heresies and Apostasy (May 2019) (vaticanCatholic.com)`

[13] https://www.Catholicnewsagency.com/news/255887/pope-francis-calls-for-paradigm-shift-in-theology-for-world-of-today

different Christian confessions and <u>different religions openly engaging with everyone, believers and nonbelievers.".",</u>" The Pope wrote in the Apostolic letter. (Author's note: This picture is what the Pope's pleasant words mean in real life. Looks like Sodom & Gomorrah to me.) [14] [15] (Author's note: This means we are to invite atheists to mass and change our mass to "suit their needs" BS!

4. We have the need to deal with" profound cultural transformations."

5. Revises the statutes of the Pontifical Academy of Theology (PATH) "to make them more suitable for the mission our time imposes on theology.

6. Theology can only develop in a culture of dialogue and encounter between different traditions and different knowledge, between different Christian confessions and different religions. Openly engaging with everyone, believers, and nonbelievers," the pope wrote in the apostolic letter.

7. Pope Francis wrote Catholic theology must experience a" courageous cultural revolution." In order to become a fundamentally contextual theology" guided by Christo's incarnation into time and space.

8. This approach to theology must be capable of reading and interpreting" the gospel in the conditions in which men and women live daily, in different geographical social and cultural environments."

---

[14] Pope participates in circus act during general audience - YouTube Note: This picture is exactly what our Blessed Mother Mary meant when she said the following when Pope said that the anti-Christ is now on earth. "He should know. He IS the anti-Christ." Can you picture Jesus Christ behaving like what this picture shows? Of course NOT!

[15] https://YouTube/wiJGPRHkjgl

9. Our Pope contrasts this approach with the current theology that has lasted for 2000 years by the way to abstractly repropose formulas and schemes from the past and repeated long-standing criticism of "deskbound theology." (In other words, "out with the old and in with the new, whatever that might be."

10. Pope Francis emphasized theological studies must be open to the world.

11. Pope Francis emphasizes that this bottoms up revisioning of theology is necessary to better aid the Churches evangelizing image.

12. Pope Francis went on to say that the new theological studies must be open to the world not as a tactical attitude but as a profound turning point which must be "inductive." (This phrase is much like what Barack Obama said running for president when he keeps repeating "hope and change!" What we got was "identity politics" that still to this day rips apart racial relationships in our country! Many words sound good right up until you understand what they really mean.

13. The new Catholicism must become transdisciplinary, part of a web of relationships. First of all, with other disciplines and other knowledge. The Pope said this engagement leads to the arduous task of theologians making use of "new categories developed by other knowledge."

14. Pope Francis wrote priority must be given to the" knowledge of people's common sense". Which he described as a "theological source in which many images of God live come often not corresponding to the Christian face of God, only and always love."

15. The Pope said His pastoral stamp must be placed upon all Catholic theology described as "popular theology."

16. Pope Francis being a heretic.

17.   Introduced a Pagan God as a substitute for Blessed Mother Mary.

He placed Pachamama idols in various places throughout the Vatican and they wound up and various cathedrals around the world as well. Pachamama is a Peruvian Inca/Indies earth Goddess and is as Pagan as you can get. It is called idolatry promoted by Pope Francis.

18.   There are many more examples of Pope Francis being nothing more than a Pagan God witch doctor.

First, did you notice anything strange in the previous eighteen points? You should have! The above text is taken straight from Christian News Agency with an article written by Jonathan Told last year in November 2023. Are you sure you did not notice anything missing from all these wonderful nicety kind words and goals regarding the entire Catholic Church? **Answer*: The name of Almighty God is missing*.** It is completely absent. This is not an accident or an oversight. It is on purpose. Leaving God out of all of these theological changes the Pope wants to make certainly without a shadow of a doubt points toward the direction he wants to take the Catholic Church. Simply put, Pope Francis wants to have a Church that looks like a Church, but it is not a Church.

19.   He wants to have celebrations like mass but not be mass. In other words, he wants a completely false Church that is worth absolutely nothing. It will be a fake Church a Church with no substance come with no Almighty Father in Heaven, with no Lord and savior Jesus Christ and without anything else that is right and good. This has been Satan's goal for an exceedingly long time. Ever since Satan saw the throne of our Almighty Father he wanted to sit in that throne. Because he felt he was

better than our Heavenly Father and deserved to be there more than anything else. As our Heavenly Father s Anointed Messenger, I have had occasion to be attacked by Satan on three separate occasions back when I was in my thirties. Satan hates me so bad it goes beyond any kind of description with any kind of language used by the human race. I outlined my encounters with Him on three separate occasions in a different part of this book.

20. I wish the picture shown below was some kind of fake or something. The horrifying truth is the picture with Pope Benedict sitting in the middle is real. Obviously, the artist whoever that Satanist is wanted to depict not the tree of life

Skeletonized Dead Jesus and The Papal Anti-Christ Pope Snake

but the tree of death. Featured in the geographic center is a disgusting depiction of our Lord and savior Jesus Christ in the form of skin and bones. The artist depicted the head of Jesus as half human and half reptile if you look close enough. Additionally, you will see strange what looks like skeletal little children climbing around the dead tree.

To the right of the skeletal Jesus, you will see a spinal cord jutting out from behind Jesus. And then in all his glory is Pope Benedict. What in the hell is going on in the Vatican to have this within one hundred miles of Rome, much less on earth and inside the Vatican on an invitation basis no less! There is no getting around the fact that it is this kind of Satanic debauchery is floating around the Vatican these days. I am surprised the Pope and others like him in the Vatican have been as successful as they are in keeping their horns from poking out of their heads. The Vatican desperately needs a colossal theological enema! That starts at the TOP!

The symbolism of the above picture is multi-dimensional and demonic from top to bottom. It has Satan written all over it. You see Christ with <u>half his head looking like an alligator</u>. Next to that, you see a <u>stylized human spine</u>. All the limbs of the tree are dead. There are caricatures of small children around. There is another crocodile in the mix. They purposely chose the lowest forms of life on earth and set them beside the highest form of life, our lord and savior Jesus Christ. All of this was done on purpose with malice and forethought aimed directly at our beloved Catholic Church

If the tree of death wasn't bad enough the welcoming hall for guests is shaped like a snake inside and out. Remember everything rotten that happened to the human race had its source as a vile dishonest snake that approached Eve in the garden of Eden. Our Heavenly Father told me personally this is TRUE! Yes! I heard His voice and that is exactly what He said to me!

21. Our Pope wants to honor the Satanic snake. To me, this is absolute proof that Anti-Christ Pope Francis it is exactly that, a Satanic Anti-Christ Pope.

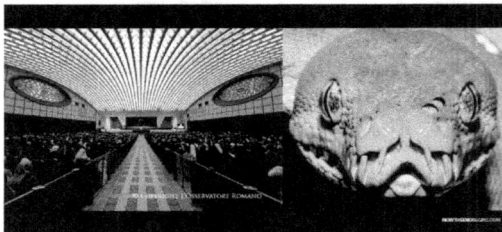

I know you don't want to beelieve this and I didn't either. But how many times do we need to get hit on our heads with indisputable proof Francis according to <u>Father Altman and others is actually not a Pope. Because of his inner beliefs that are not Catholic at all,</u> and he parades around with scantily clad female circus performers and has the welcoming hall designed as a snake to honor Satan. Yes, that's right, Pope Francis honors Satan. Get used to that thought because it is the damned truth. I am so hot and angry about this you could probably fry an egg on the top of my head.

22. Priests can now bless same sex couples. Would our Heavenly Father do that?

23. All this is coming from a Pope who said some time ago people could disappear and God can make new species. An interview with Eugenio Scafari. In Italy.

24. The Pope said if a person is in hell and then they feel sorry for their deeds they will not be punished. They willll be forgiven and be with God. Those who are not sorry will just stop existing.

25. The Pope does not believe in hell. Those who do bad things just disappear.

26. It is reported the Pope also said people should stop trying to make people Catholics. That is silly.

27. There is no particular Catholic God, only God.

28. Priests could forgive women that had an abortion

29. It is now acceptable to mix Catholic Christianity with other religions like Islam or Buddaism and so on.

30. Lastly pope francis attacks the center peace of our faith – he now questions the birth, death and ressuraction of jesus christ! He also eliminates the name of jesus christ. Read below please

7

Pope Francis Claims Jesus's Death Is Not What We are Being Told [16]

I do not understand what the Pope is talking about if he really means the death of our Lord and Savior Jesus Christ is NOT what we are being told. Well, YES, it is. Francis has been talking about what he calls, "the true nature of Jesus death." Like we did not know during the past 2,024 years. Gee, thousands of people have been studying that for 2000 years! But Francis is now claiming they have all missed the point.

This having salute me tyrannical and pompous statement goes against frankly everything in the New Testament. Francis is doing everything he can to confuse and create chaos regarding the foundational teachings of the Catholic Church. Remember my dear sacred child of God one of the tactics of Satan is to create confusion and chaos. This is precisely what Pope Francis is trying to do.

No, we have not. This video acts as if we are ignorant about the life and teachings of Jesus. Christians always use Jesus as the Blessed Shining Example on a Hill providing the perfect example on how to live our lives. Perhaps the Pope does not understand the laity as well as he thinks.

In the above document, what Pope Francis wants to bring everybody together is to throw out the Bible and the Christian mass that has served us for more than 2,000 years. And replace it with an amalgamation of different religions from around the world that will certainly end up being very secular with no mention of Almighty God.

---

[16] Pope Francis Reveals That Jesus's Death Is NOT What We're Being Told (youtube.com) https://www.youtube.com/watch?v=mO9cMyILTJM

This is the biggest Satanic fraud I have ever run across in my life. This is pure Satan from the top of His head to the end of His tail.

What exactly did Pope Francis say?

In an interview recorded in footnote number 17, this is a summary some of it repetitive of what he said.

1. Catholic priests can bless same-sex couples. Francis squirmed around this by saying they can bless each separate member of the gay couple but not the marriage itself. *That is stinking lawyer talk not theological. Leviticus 20:13, 1 Corinthians 6:9, there are many more.*

2. Humans can disappear and God can create new species. *This is right out of pagan mysticism*

3. Regarding sin, people who have committed grave sins if they say they are sorry for their sins God will allow them into heaven just like all the other faithful sacred children of our heavenly father. *This is blatantly false for the act of sin is without any doubt a rejection of our Almighty father and his specific rules we are to follow while we are on the earth. The unforgivable sin is rejection of our heavenly father through acts of sin. This shows the satanic influence that is embedded in Pope Francis.*

4. The Pope said the biggest problems in the world are our young people not having jobs and old people feeling lonely. *Really? Has this Pope totally forgotten about although hatred and wars going on right now? Has he forgotten all the murders and all the financial cheating and all the dishonesty, the telling of lies politicians lying so as to gain more power and money? The Pope has completely forgotten about the horrific actions of Satan. Of course, he would because he is controlled by Satan and is indeed the Antichrist sitting on the throne of St. Peter.*

5. The Pope actually said that trying to make other people Catholics does not make any sense and is silly. *Really? Jesus Christ is the way the truth and the life and no one goes to the Father except by Him. Pope Francis has just rejected all of*

Catholicism and one of its foundational principles of evangelism and spreading the word of the Bible and God. According to Francis I should not bother writing theological books that are heavenly father has asked me directly to do. Only Satan would say such a thing.

6. Regarding abortions he said priests can absolve women who had abortions. *So, it's okay with the Pope to kill innocent developing sacred children of God when they're still in the womb. Just go to confession.*

7. The rich and the poor must have equal and fair lives. *This strongly implies a monster government to redistribute the wealth created by the few to the many. Socialism which only equally distributes poverty which has been proven many times in the past on this earth. It has been proven that every scheme of socialism or communism ends in complete disaster and horrific suffering for all the people. But this is exactly what Satan wants which is to destroy all of God's sacred children made in his image. Francis is promoting these filthy Satanic ideas.*

8. Divorced people who remarry can have communion. *Your marriage must be annulled by the church before you can receive the sacrament of communion.*

9. Francis is attempting to redefine what is right and wrong where instead of objective definitions of what is right and wrong he says it needs to be reconciled with the individual. *In other words, it is up to the individual to decide for themselves what is right and wrong. Adolf Hitler thought what he was doing was right and millions of people died as a result. Pope Francis does not mention this inconvenient fact. Another satanic attempt at confusing God's sacred children on earth.*

10. He thinks priests should marry. *This is one of the few things that separate the laity from the priesthood. Dissolving this end up dissolving the Catholic church. Why wouldn't he say that*

considering he is the antichrist and does indeed want to destroy God's sacred children and the church at Satan's command.

11. The teachings of the church must basically bend with the social wins in a culture or society. *Gone will be the thought that the church represents immutable and unchangeable rules of Almighty God for the benefit of human existence or more accurately put the sacred children of our heavenly father. Francis forgets that there are 10 Commandments not 10 suggestions from our heavenly and loving father. These commandments were specifically given to his sacred children on earth so that if they obeyed these commandments their lives on earth will be far happier and productive with no violence. Francis does not like that. Here is Satan yet again.*

12. Nothing is beyond forgiveness. *Forget the unforgivable sin which is the rejection of Almighty God as demonstrated by a sinful life devoid of prayer and worship. It is a person's life that determines the rejection or the acceptance of our heavenly father. Those who reject our heavenly father will pass through the gates of hell, never heaven.*

13. Addressing inmates at a prison the Pope said, "everyone can slip." *Everyone? Really? No! The Pope means to say that criminals in jail are no different than everyone else and anyone can make a mistake. A mistake is defined as intending to do something that didn't turn out as intended. All crime is intentional! Worse yet this idiocy sanctifies criminal behavior and gives dignity to criminals when he completed his sentence and saying Jesus wants it this way. This is pure BS! The Pope is a criminal apologist and not a Pope!*

14. Pope Francis talks about the "failure of the cross." *This means that Jesus failed in his mission to redeem God's sacred children and reconcile their state of original sin from Adam and Eve with our heavenly father. Remember please, Jesus Christ is fully God and therefore pure and perfect in every way. It is impossible for*

Jesus to fail at anything. This stinking proclamation is further proof that Francis desperately wants to destroy the Catholic faith, the Christian faith and the church founded by our Lord and Savior Jesus Christ. Francis is conducting a direct attack against Almighty God, his only begotten son and Lord and Savior of this world, and the Holy Spirit which proceeds from them. When Francis dies, he certainly will have to face Jesus and then he will be shown the doors of hell through which he will go.

Please read the following text below and see what our blessed mother Mary has to say regarding this point of what Francis said about the cross and Jesus.

While reading the above did you find the word God anywhere? Well, it is not there. The above is nothing more than a man centered theology where humankind worships itself. This is the biggest

Remember, fish liked the taste of the worm right before they were caught and killed. Same thing here, most people do not know the definitions of the words that are used in the above trash heap of liberal woke communist ideas. This is basically the Vatican trying to have people seeing the theological version of kumbaya around the campfire.

Question: My dearest Mother Mary, I just read this pathetic theological mess proposed by our Anti-Christ Francis. To me the message is as plain as can be. This will mean the destruction of the Church founded by your Son and my Savior Jesus Christ. This is pure Satan disguised as fancy and ambiguous words that sound good to people with low IQ's.

Pope Francis Reveals Jesus's Death Is NOT What We're Being Told (youtube.com)

It appears to me pretty simple. They want to take Christianity and nail it together with other unnamed religions at this point so that the new so-called religion will better serve the needs of the population that wants to adore itself. God is completely eliminated from everything.

Mankind simply wants to worship itself and this is the way they want to do it. Now I understand and more depth why our Father in Heaven wants to bring the end of the world as we know it. I am completely disgusted. Dear Mother Mary, I know this must be treacherously painful for you what I would very much like your comments and anything you would like to say about this.

Answer: *Oh, my dear son, you definitely have accurately characterized this awful attempt by Satan to fool all of God's sacred children. You have accurately surmised that <u>this will result in the extinction of our Church and our sacraments and the mass as well</u>. Your lifelong friend has said this for years and he is correct.*

I guess there is no sense in me commenting on each individual thorn of the thorn bush because in the end <u>this Satanic scheme will overtake all good Christians unless they hide</u>. We knew of course this was coming and <u>I knew that Francis would be the antipope</u>, the Pope under the control of Satan. This has come to pass.

Frankly, my dearest of sons I don't know what else to tell you that you haven't already surmised yourself. You will be protected from the very dark times that are just right around the corner. Just follow the directions from your Lord and savior and my son and you and your family will do fine.

My dearest of sons, I love you ever so much.
Your Blessed Mother Mary

April 29, 2024

My dearest Blessed Mother Mary, this section of your book is the most painful thing I have ever had to write in my entire life. As you know, I have known for some time that this kind of thing would happen. But to actually see the ugly face of it makes me want to throw up. You're just like being near an erupting volcano and watching the lava come rushing toward you knowing you could never outrun it. It is such a miserable feeling of helplessness. And on top of it almost all of its future victims go about their daily lives completely oblivious to the maelstrom that is heading their way and overtake them very quickly now.

Dear Mother, I know you have experienced much of this before and frankly I don't know how you do it. To watch these miserable things, occur when if only people paid attention to your apparitions most of it would have never happened. It makes me sick to my stomach and frankly as a confession anger is boiling up inside me and I am truly short-tempered, now. That's not like me but there it is.

So many people in their future will label the coming events as the wrath of God or God's anger punishing the people. That is ever so wrong because our loving Father Is the purest love I have ever experienced in my life. Our Holy Father is simply removing His protection from mankind so natural Satanic occurrences will now be set free. Thank you for listening to this my dear Blessed Mother Mary. I would so very much like to hear any additional thoughts you may have dear Mother Mary. I love you.

April 29, 2024
8:33 AM

Blessed Mother Mary: *My dearest of sons, it breaks my Heart to see you suffer so badly as I know you are. You are in a very lonely position where there is nobody around you that comes close to understanding what the depth is of your understanding and the emotional impact it has on you. Yet my dearest of sons both Jesus and I see within you with that fighter that will not hesitate to single-handedly go up against an army Satan.*

My dear son, Satan knows this of you, and he will steer clear of you because you will defeat Him in any arena of battle. <u>There will come a time when you speak to many people at once and you will be opposed by minions of Satan</u>. I know you will have No Fear because of your eloquence, your intelligence, your knowledge, and most of all your love for the Trinity and me. You will dispatch them and there, as you would say, cockamamie arguments that result in Satanic domination *and suffering. <u>You will feel like you are very alone but as you know that is impossible with you.</u>*

At this point my dear son, just work on the other sections of this book, and finish them with my help and then let it be published. From there contact the various Christian organizations and ensure they get a copy of this life changing miraculous book. They will want to talk to you then what you tell the truth to them they will be amazed and far better off for having heard what you say.

<u>By the way, my dear son, when I say that you are protected, I should tell you that not only are my Son and I right by your right side. But both of us now also have our left arms resting on your shoulders. This keeps Satan away from you and any others of His condemned minions. Besides that, there are two angels now with you. There is one on the left and one on the right there is no way that Satan can touch you from now till the time that you join us.</u>

The love for you is so great within the Heavenly Kingdom. I know this is hard to believe but there are now millions that pray for you and are always asking your Father to protect you in all ways during your remaining time on earth. There are other sections in this book that are still incomplete, and I just want you to finish those expeditiously and then send it to your publishing company Advantage Publishing. Mike loves you and feels privileged not only to know you but also to publish your books. That grace of God is with you ever so much.

Your Loving Blessed Mother Mary

Thank You So Very Much Dear Mother Mary
I Love you

8

Blessed Mother Mary Told Me Pope Francis Is Indeed the Anti-Christ. He Is Under Control of Satan.

Much more detail in the previous Booklet, "Blessed Mother Mary Reveals Her Apparitions" when our Blessed Mother Mary describes the third secret of Fatima in great detail. I strongly suggest you not pay attention to other writings about the 3rd secret because the air is polluted with false accounts. The Pope himself lied about it. The secret exposes great sins committed by the Vatican. The Vatican went to far as to hide the real Sister Lucia and put a fake Sister Lucia in her place. Someone who agreed to promote the lies of the Vatican.

Can a Pope Be Controlled by Satan?

Yes! He already is. Blessed Mother Mary has perfect and pure knowledge of the situation with the Catholic Church, and it is Her who told me this on several occasions and that is published within this book. Please put all the pieces together, all the heresies and the two pictures shown here. There are many more pictures of occult statues inside the Vatican and those of Pope Francis holding religious objects he NEVER should as a genuine Pope. [17]

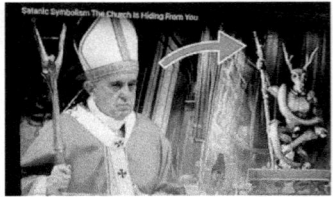

---

[17] Satanic Symbolism the Church Is Hiding from You - YouTube

Question: Dear Blessed Mother Mary, would you care to comment on the extent of Satanic activities within the Vatican these days? Father Malachi Martin acknowledged all this is going on and it is worse than we normally would think of. If there is something you would like to illuminate for us, I would be very grateful if you could do that.

Answer: *My dearest sacred child, you are so exhausted and tired right now so I will keep my answer very concise and short. As you already suspect the Satanic gremlins are scurrying about within the Vatican each doing its part to bring the whole house down. That is probably the best way to explain the situation. They are indeed working towards the time when Satan himself will arrive and he will sit on the throne of Peter. That will happen inside the Vatican where the Pope normally sits. This is something Satan craved for his entire existence. Since he tried to overthrow your Heavenly Father and was instantly defeated. And kicked out of the Kingdom thrown down to earth to be a pest for everyone who comes here that are your Father's sacred children. The people in the Vatican that are not Satanic live their lives in fear. They know if they say one wrong thing their lifetime of dedication and work toward our Heavenly Father will be instantly thrown in the garbage. And they will then be severely chastised and most likely transferred far away from Rome to where the Pope thinks they cannot do any harm to his Satanic plans. I know this is awful dear son for you to hear but I also know that frankly you already knew every word that I just said. I love you so very much my dearest. I ask please that you quit out for the night because I sense that your head is really hurting from yet another headache that tortures you so frequently. I love you, your Blessed Mother.*

Remember my dearest sacred children of our Heavenly Father, Cardinal Bergoglio now known as the Pope was there originally from Argentina. That country is very communist socialist and its governmental nature. That form of government which frankly saps the economic blood out of all of God's children who live there is what are now Pope thinks is a wonderful thing. That form of government is tyrannical and dictatorial and is what our Pope thinks is normal. It certainly is not for governments that are so opposed to serve the best interest of the people and not dictate to them with threats of violence and jail time if they misbehave. This picture illustrates the sickness of our Pope when he adores looking at a communist cross. It is made of a sickle and hammer with Jesus Christ our Lord and savior being crucified on the hammer. Do not think for a moment that the symbolism of communism reigning supreme over Jesus Christ can be ignored by this wretched hammer and sickle. [18]

---

[18] Satanic Symbolism the Church is Hiding from You - YouTube

9

The New Satanic Horrors Instigated from Cardinal Bergoglio, aka. Pope Francis

In that form of government falsehoods and manipulation it is a normal course of events in the government's attempts to control every aspect of our Heavenly Father's sacred children who live there. We here in the United States are now experiencing more and more of this atrocity through the efforts of the Democrat party and the Joe Biden administration.

Among the many other things Pope Francis has instituted that are Satanic, he is instituting the following: *Ad Theologian Promovendam. It means from Latin,* "to promote theology." This sounds innocent enough does it not? It is not!

Pope Francis calls for 'paradigm shift' in theology for world of today [19] *These are fancy words that can mean anything. But what it does mean is that the Vatican under the control of Pope Francis wants to run away from the original Catholic teachings. That were handed down through the centuries. That originated with Jesus Christ himself. Jesus is the Trinity. One microbe definition of the Trinity is as follows: the Trinity is one made up of three. The three are one. One in three and three in one. Each member of the Trinity is infinite in his own right. Before each of us was born at the wish of our heavenly father, the Trinity would be completely fulfilled by exploring the infinite character of each of the other two infinite beings within the Trinity. However, our heavenly father wished to expand their*

---

[19] https://www.Catholicnewsagency.com/news/255887/pope-francis-calls-for-paradigm-shift-in-theology-for-world-of-today

fulfillment and enjoyment by creating sacred children in their own image. That is us. All of us were given the sacred gift of free will because our heavenly father wanted all of his sacred children to love him voluntarily exercising their individual gift of free will.

There is a more complete explanation of this in the first major book written by me with Jesus Christ himself. The title is, **"God's Grand Design of All Creation for Your Redemption***." This can also be found in the first booklet written titled,* **"God's Grand Design, Creation, Booklet 1***"*

There are many more heresies instigated by Pope Francis. Due to page limitations, I cannot include all of the wretched Satanic activities of Pope Francis.

I pray for my children and especially for my grandchildren. For they will live through the End of Times propagated by Satan Himself who by the way knows me very well and I know Satan very well. How can that be? 50 years ago, Satan personally attacked me in the middle of the night while I was sleeping next to my Blessed wife. I have documented this in detail in other writings. He said to me" I will get you! I will get you! I will get you! Yes, Satan does indeed have red eyes and is about seven feet tall. He sure is an ugly bastard.

What you are about to read eliminates Almighty God and Christianity and all our Biblical literature. Replaced by mankind worshiping and adoring mankind.

Pope Francis is calling for a paradigm shift where Catholic theology takes a much broader view of engagement with the world that includes contemporary science, modern culture throughout the earth, and people's lived experiences.

Boy, doesn't this sound so good! The Satanic team of Francis is going to reconcile Biblical teachings with science that changes all the time. Due to new discoveries. He wants to blend Biblical teachings with our perverted modern culture that includes, abortion on demand, gay marriages, men turning into women and occupying women's locker rooms.

Who will pay for all of this Satanic garbage in our society? If you work for an honest living, it is YOU!! For certain there will be monstrous tax hikes the likes of which we have never seen before. One note about taxes. When people go to work, they purposely invest part of their life to earn the money necessary to support the needs of a family. It is a simple trade. I trade part of my life to provide the necessary items to be purchased for my loving family.

Because of the coming taxes, the amount of your life taken away will increase from five-twelfths (according to the latest government statistics) of a year to my personal estimated eight months out of each year. That is called slavery. Honest people that work will become working slaves. Yes, this is my personal estimate and does not come from any accredited institution. I simply used common sense. Common sense sadly appears to be more and more rare as time goes on.

One World Government and Religion

1. One world government,

2. One world judicial system,

3. One world religious theology Pagan based with NO Catholicism make the Bible illegal and replace it with the new catastrophic man-made stench of garbage that is founded upon the principles of Sodom and Gomorrah. It will be a document of mankind worshipping mankind!

4. Possession of a Bible will be illegal.

5. Complete control of food distribution,

6. A one-world police replacement. There will come a time when simply possessing a Bible will be deemed a crime.

7. Conducting our sacred mass will also become a crime against the state.

8. Godly human rights out the window

More From Cardinal Bergoglio aka. Pope Francis

1. On May 20, 2024, Fox News Stuart Varny Show, they reported Pope Francis said over the weekend, "conservative Bishops that oppose blessing same sex marriages have a "suicidal attitude". This goes directly against 2,000 years of Church teachings since Saint Peter was given the leadership if the Catholic Church directly from Jesus Christ Himself! It is clear from this the Pope wants to destroy the Catholic Church.

2. A new document titled <u>Ad Theologian</u> Comes from the Pontifical Academy of Theology. This "theology can only develop in a culture of dialogue and encounter between different traditions and different knowledge. And between different Christian confessions and different religions openly engaging with everyone, believers and non-believers," the Pope wrote in the Apostolic letter.

   This odor of dead fish basically means our divine gospel will now be mixed in with other religions on earth. This is impossible especially when it comes to Islam. The goal of Islam is earthly domination over everyone. The goal of our loving gospel is to spread God's words and serve the needs of all others of God's sacred children. Simply put that they want to combine a religion that seeks worldly domination with every religion that seeks love and justice for all of God's sacred children. These two can never be reconciled. Why? <u>Because one is of God and the other is of Satan</u>.

3. We have the need to deal with" profound cultural transformations.

   The above phrase is a code for creating Sodom and Gomorrah in our societies. Notice it never says what our societies will transform into. That is left open to the Satanic minions that will sit down and create a new social disaster of monumental proportion.

4. Revises the statutes of the Pontifical Academy of Theology (PATH) "to make them more suitable for the mission that our time imposes on theology.

   More purposeful ambiguous garbage. This is a feel-good meaningless phrase. The keywords though are "the mission that our time imposes on theology." The world is a theological disaster area, it lacks the necessary principles of, "love God first, love your neighbor as your love yourself and love your enemy." Our times today have drifted far away from the will of Almighty God, yet this phrase opens the door to let the stink of immorality invade the new and improved theology." By the way, this new so-called theology is worldwide. There will be one and only one worldwide theology and only one religion. All other religions will certainly be deemed as illegal.

5. Theology can only develop in a culture of dialogue and encounter between different traditions and different knowledge. And between different Christian confessions and different religions, openly engaging with everyone, believers, and nonbelievers," the pope wrote in the apostolic letter.

   Good God! Theology development? The word development directly means creating a new theology. Get that real well dear sacred child! They wish to create a new theology that must by its very nature throw away our Godly inspired Biblical literature and replace it with and amalgamation (mixture) of other religious texts from around the world. Dear sacred children of God: our beloved Bible will be thrown out and its replacement is something that we will never understand because it is Satanically unbiblical.

6. Pope Francis wrote Catholic theology must experience a" courageous cultural revolution." In order to become a fundamentally contextual theology" guided by Christo's incarnation into time and space.

   A courageous cultural revolution. This phrase says that the new religion will be integrated with our culture, thus it will never be the same again. Today, there were multiple cultures that live under the umbrella of Christianity. This will go away with the newly dictated one world religion. This is what the above fancy ambiguous words mean.

7. This approach to theology must be capable of reading and interpreting" the gospel in the conditions in which men and women live daily, in different geographical social and cultural environments."

Whew! To most rational intelligent people the above sentence looks innocent yet completely not understandable. But it contains code words that do have specific meanings. The new theology must be the lowest common denominator of people around the world. These people think they can create one singular document with that combines the worldview of Aborigines, African tribesmen, Muslims, and Christians altogether into one happy pot of people singing kumbaya. And never will they mention Almighty God, the creator of all that is seen and unseen.

8. Our beloved Pope contrasts this approach with the current theology that has lasted for 2000 years by the way to abstractly repropose formulas and schemes from the past and repeated long-standing criticism of "deskbound theology."

This phrase is among the most ambiguous of all. He thinks current theology is born out of a desk in the room somewhere. Apparently, he has paid no attention to His own magisterium in Rome. At this point reaffirms what I have already said that Pope Francis wants to throw everything out that mankind has achieved in our theological understandings then replace it with their one world religion. That is enforced by an army of censers

9. Pope Francis emphasized that theological studies must be open to the world.

Looks like everybody in the world will have to take indoctrination classes. This is exactly what Kim Il Sung, Mao Zedong, Joseph Stalin, Fidel Castro, and the current leader of North Korea.

10. Pope Francis emphasizes that this bottoms up envisioning of theology is necessary to better aid the Churches evangelizing image.

Our Satanic Pope wants us to believe that it is the people that will decide about theological principles. He wants the people to "re-envision," what they want to believe in. Notice dear sacred children of God, there is not one mention of our Heavenly Father creator of Heaven and earth. This re-envisioning (what an intelligent sounding word, re envisioning) means nothing more than pulling theology out of your imagination. This is yet again another way for mankind to adore and love itself. This is what the people that lived in Sodom and Gomorrah did. They invented God's out of their imagination. They worshipped Gods that they themselves created. They had ritual killings of small children. I implore you; I beg you to look up Sodom and Gomorrah in a reliable source that has not already been tainted with liberal progressive positions. This is pure Satanism and exactly what Satan wants God's children to do. And Pope Francis is doing it.

11. Pope Francis went on to say that the new theological studies must be open to the world not as a tactical attitude but as a profound turning point which must be "inductive."

This is the most nonsensical sentence that I have ever run into in my entire life. However, if you take the phrase "a profound turning point which must be inductive," the word inductive means to gather up and make inclusive. This is the word that was used during World War II when millions of men were inducted into the army against their will. This phrase could very easily mean that the turning point in theology must include inducting people against their will. This would be consistent with cardinal Bergoglio's communist worldview. You know the cardinal; he is now the Pope.

12. The new Catholicism must become transdisciplinary, part of a web of relationships. First of all, with other disciplines and

other knowledge. The Pope said this engagement leads to the arduous task of theologians making use of "new categories developed by other knowledge."

I think this is pretty obvious. The word transdisciplinary means: Welcoming the different lenses that each person brings to the table makes the decision-making process richly transdisciplinary. When it comes to theology however, the word theology means the study of God. These people never mentioned God. They want to bring together a number of people that will decide theological principles that makes everybody happy. This is another form of mankind adoring and loving itself. This is like the political slogan from Barack Obama, hope and change. I'm sure they paid the marketing guy a lot of money to come up with that one.

13. Pope Francis wrote priority must be given to the" knowledge of people's common sense". Which he described as a" theological source in which many images of God live often not corresponding to the Christian face of God, only and always love."

This phrase is a mixture of underlying communist worldview along with a perverted view of Almighty God that specifically rejects Almighty God as we know Him now. Our Heavenly Father never changes but this idiot phrase talks about the many images of God often NOT corresponding to the Christian face of God. So, this Satanic crackpot reinvent a God with many faces. So, he wants us to throw out our beloved Bible and invent a new one out of our sinful imaginations. This is an act of pure self-worship! If you take the previous sentence literally, why is it nobody has ever seen the face of God including me that has talked with Him on a number of magnificent occasions. I heard His loving voice talking to me, but I never once got a glimpse of His face.

On the other hand, if you take this phrase metaphorically then it means God's character is different depending upon the angle you are coming from.

Also remember, this phrase says we must allow non-Christian interpretations of Almighty God. Just imagine how many that could be!

14. The Pope said His pastoral stamp must be placed upon all Catholic theology described as "popular theology." Well, here we go again, Mr. Pope wants absolute authority over all things related to God.

Well, there you have it. What a great sounding batch of words that could mean anything. This is exactly what crafty dishonest politicians do. Throw together a bunch of nicely pleasant words and make it like we will have Heaven on earth according to our needs. I ask each reader to read again what is above and then definitively express the meanings of the above in clear terms.

Dear sacred children of Almighty God:

This Is Exactly What Satan Has Wanted Ever Since He Rebelled Against Our Heavenly Father in The Heavenly Kingdom. He Has Always Wanted to Replace Our Loving Father in Heaven. Read This Stinking Phrase Very Well Because What I Have Just Said Is Exactly What It Means. Jorge Mario Bergoglio Wants to Play God. And The Rest of Us Are His Servants.

First, did you notice anything strange in the previous 14 points? You should have! The above text is taken straight from Christian news agency with an article written by Jonathan Told last year in November 2023. Are you sure you didn't notice anything missing from all these wonderful goals regarding the entire Catholic Church?

The name of Almighty God is missing. It is completely absent. This is not an accident or an oversight. It is on purpose. It can only be a Pope controlled by Satan that would do such a miserable thing to all the faithful who attend Church every Sunday. Leaving God out of all of these theological changes the Pope wants to make certainly without a shadow of a doubt points toward the direction he wants to take the Catholic Church.

Simply put, Pope Francis wants to have a Church that looks like a Church, but it is not a Church. He wants to have celebrations like mass but not be mass. In other words, he wants a completely false Church that is worth absolutely nothing. It will be a fake Church a Church with no substance come with no Almighty Father in Heaven, with no Lord and savior Jesus Christ and without anything else that is right and good. This has been Satan's goal for an exceptionally long time. Ever since Satan saw the throne of our Almighty Father he wanted to sit in that throne because he felt he was better than our Heavenly Father and deserved to be there above all else.

As our Heavenly Father s Anointed Messenger, I have had occasion to encounter Satan on three separate occasions back when I was in my thirties. Satan hates me so bad it goes beyond any kind of description with any kind of language used by the human race. I outlined my encounter with Him on three separate occasions. After that, Satan has harassed me every day of my life.

In the above summary document, Pope Francis wants to bring everybody together is fundamentally throw out the Bible. And throw out Christian mass that has served us well for more than 2000 years. And replace it with an amalgamation of different religions from around the world that will certainly end up being very secular with no mention of Almighty God.

While reading the above did you find the word God anywhere? Well, it is not there. The above is nothing more than a man centered theology where mankind worships itself. This is the biggest Satanic fraud I have ever run across in my life. This is pure Satan from the top of His head to the end of His tail.

Remember, fish liked the taste of the worm right before they were caught and killed. Same thing here, most people do not know the definitions of the words that are used in the above trash heap of liberal woke communist theological ideas. This is basically trying to have people seeing the theological version of kumbaya around the campfire.

Question: my dearest Mother Mary, I just read this pathetic theological mess proposed by our Anti-Christ Francis. To me the message is as plain as can be. This will mean the destruction of the Church founded by your son and my savior Jesus Christ. This is pure Satan disguised as fancy and ambiguous words that sound good to people with low IQ's.

It appears to me pretty simple. They want to take Christianity and mailed it together with other unnamed religions at this point so that the new so-called religion will better serve the needs of the population that wants to adore itself. God is completely eliminated from everything. Mankind simply wants to worship itself and this is the way they want to do it. Now I understand and more depth why our Father in Heaven wants to bring the end of the world as we know it. I am completely disgusted. Dear Mother Mary, I know this must be treacherously painful for you what I would very much like your comments and anything you would like to say about this.

Answer: *Oh, my dear son, you definitely have accurately characterized this awful attempt by Satan to fool all of God's sacred children. You have accurately surmised that this will result in the extinction of our Church and our sacraments and the mass as well. Your lifelong friend has said this for years and he is correct.*

I guess there is no sense in me commenting on each individual thorn of the thorn bush because in the end this Satanic scheme will overtake all good Christians unless they hide. We knew of course this was coming and I knew that Francis would be the antipope, the Pope under the control of Satan. This has come to pass.

Frankly, my dearest of sons, I don't know what else to tell you that you haven't already surmised yourself. You will be protected from the very dark times that are just right around the corner. Just follow the directions from your Lord and savior and my son and you and your family will do fine.

My dearest of sons,
I love you ever so much.
Your Blessed Mother Mary

April 29, 2024

My dearest Blessed Mother Mary, this section of your book is the most painful thing I have ever had to write in my entire life. As you know, I have known for some time that this kind of thing would happen. But to actually see the ugly face of it makes me want to throw up. You're just like being near an erupting volcano and watching the lava come rushing toward you knowing you could never outrun it. It is such a miserable feeling of helplessness. And on top of it almost all of its future victims go about their daily lives completely oblivious to the maelstrom that is heading their way and overtake them very quickly now.

Dear Blessed Mother, I know you have experienced much of this before and frankly I don't know how you do it. To watch these miserable things, occur when if only people paid attention to your apparitions most of it would have never happened. It makes me sick to my stomach and frankly as a confession anger is boiling up inside me and I'm truly short-tempered, now. That's not like me but there it is.

So many people in their future will label the coming events as the wrath of God or God's anger punishing the people. That is ever so wrong because our loving Father Is the purest love I have ever experienced in my life. Our Holy Father is simply removing His protection from mankind so natural Satanic occurrences will now be set free. Thank you for listening to this my dear Blessed Mother Mary. I would so very much like to hear any additional thoughts you may have dear Mother Mary. I love you.

April 29, 2024
8:33 AM

My dearest of sons, it breaks my Heart to see you suffer so badly as I know you are. You are in a very lonely position where there is nobody around you that comes close to understanding what the depth is of your understandings and the emotional impact it has on you. Yet my dearest of sons both Jesus and I see within you with that fighter that will not hesitate to single-handedly go up against an army Satan.

My dear son, Satan knows this of you, and he will steer clear of you because you will defeat Him in any arena of battle. There will come a time when you will speak to many people at once and you will be opposed by minions of Satan. I know you will have No Fear because of your eloquence, your intelligence, your knowledge, and most of all your love for the Trinity and me. You will dispatch them and there, as you would say, cockamamie arguments that result in Satanic domination and suffering. You will feel like you are very alone but as you know that is impossible with you.

At this point my dear son, just work on the other sections of this book, and finish them with my help and then let it be published. From there contact the various Christian organizations and ensure they get a copy of this life changing miraculous book. They will want to talk to you then what you tell the truth to them they will be amazed and far better off for having heard what you say.

By the way, my dear son. When I say that you are protected, I should tell you that not only are my Son and I right by your right side. But both of us now also have our left arms resting on your shoulders. This keeps Satan away from you and any others of His condemned minions. Besides that, there are two angels now with you. There is one on the left and one on the right there is no way that Satan can touch you from now till the time that you join us.

The love for you is so great within the Heavenly Kingdom. I know this is hard to believe but there are now millions that pray for you and are always asking your Father to protect you in all ways during your remaining time on earth. There are other sections in this book that are still incomplete, and I just want you to finish those expeditiously and then send it to your publishing company Advantage Publishing. Mike loves you and feels privileged not only to know you but also to publish your books. That grace of God is with you ever so much.

Your Loving Blessed Mother Mary

10

The Heresies of Pope Francis

This next section is horrid, it is disgusting, it is Satanic, and it goes against all Biblical literature as we know it today. If there is any doubt in your mind Pope Francis is not the Anti-Christ then you must believe two things:

1. You must just believe our Blessed Mother Mary. That when she said in this book that Pope Francis is the Anti-Christ

2. You must believe in anti-Christian dogma as it is spewed out from the Vatican by anti-Pope Francis these days.

I can only give you a small sampling of the theological garbage Pope Francis is spreading across the world. Because if I included everything this section of the book would be a large book in and of itself. So here are a few of the heresies and Satanic items they came from Anti-Christ Francis.

"Here, in fact, the different religious identities of Orthodox, Catholics, other Christians, Muslims and Jews. And the ethnic differences between Macedonians, Albanians, Serbs, Croats, and persons of other backgrounds, have created a mosaic in which every piece is essential for the uniqueness and beauty of the whole. That beauty will become all the more evident to the extent you succeed in passing it on and planting it in the Hearts of the coming generation. Every effort made to enable the diverse religious expressions…" [7]

This is blunt apostasy. The apostate Francis says that it "is essential for the uniqueness and beauty of the whole" society to have the presence of false religions, including Islam and Judaism

In plain language our apostate Pope wants to mix together all the different religions in the world into one and only one religion. This will disintegrate the Catholic Church to be something that is unrecognizable. The reason for this again is simple, this prepares the theological way for Satan to rule the world. [20]

Francis' Heresies on Atheism and Atheists:

Antipope Francis, Evangelia Gaudium (# 254), Nov. 24, 2013: "Non-Christians [such as pagans and atheists], by God's gracious initiative, when they are faithful to their own consciences, can live "justified by the grace of God". And thus be "associated to the paschal mystery of Jesus Christ" … to the sacramental dimension of sanctifying grace... to live our own beliefs."

What the above fancy worded paragraph means is God will forgive everybody no matter how rotten and cruel and Satanic they are because of His gracious initiative and them being faithful to their own conscience. This means Pope Francis believes Almighty God will forgive all the mass murderers in history as long as they were faithful to their own conscience. This also means you will be rubbing shoulders in the Heavenly Kingdom with every violent criminal that ever existed.

The Vatican II sect and Francis officially teaches one can be an atheist through no fault of His own and that atheists can be excused and saved. This is as wrong as wrong can get. The evidence of Christian morality and ethics and the existence of an Almighty God who loves us is all over the place as soon as you use your eyes to look at what's around you. The idea of evolution creating our bodies through "random selection" has been proven to be as false as false can get from a scientific viewpoint. Given our physical complexity the chances our bodies somehow evolved to what we see today is one in $1 * 10$ to the 190th power. There are not that many atoms in the whole universe.

Vatican II document, Lumen Gentium # 16: "Nor does divine providence deny the helps that are necessary for salvation to those who,

---

[20] Antipope Francis' Notable Heresies and Apostasy (May 2019) (vaticanCatholic.com)

through no fault of their own, have not yet attained to the express recognition of God. Yet, who strive, not without divine grace, to lead an upright life."

Vatican II is teaching here there are some people who, THROUGH NO FAULT OF THEIR OWN, have not yet attained the express recognition of God. In other words, there are people who, through no fault of their own, don't believe in God (i.e., are atheists). This is heresy.

The above two paragraphs exemplify the Satanic heresy of anti-Pope Francis. He loves the use the phrase "through no fault of their own." Really? Everybody is responsible for absolutely everything they ever say and do. Did the mass murderer not mean to kill all those people so therefore it is not His fault? This is the same thinking of the Democrat party in the United States.

Yet despite this dogmatic teaching based on Romans 1, in On Heaven and Earth, pp. 12-13 Francis says he respects atheists and doesn't try to convert them. He also says their "life is not condemned": So, our Anti-Christ Francis really likes atheists a lot. There is one unforgivable sin in God's creation and that is simply rejecting Almighty God. But that's okay, because Anti-Christ Francis likes them.

"I do not approach the relationship in order to proselytize or convert the atheist. I respect Him. Nor would I say His life is condemned. Because I am convinced, I do not have the right to make a judgment about the honesty of that person... every man is the image of God, whether he is a believer or not. For that reason alone, everyone has a series of virtues, qualities, and a greatness of His own." (Francis, On Heaven and Earth, pp. 12-13)

Question: would you like Anti-Christ Francis to teach your children catechism?

Answer: In contrast to Francis, the Council of Florence defined any individual with a view contrary to the Catholic Church's teaching on Our Lord Jesus Christ or the Trinity is rejected, condemned, and anathematized by God.

An atheists interviewed Francis for the Italian newspaper The Republic. The interview was published on October 1, 2013. Francis directly told the atheist he had no intention of trying to convert Him. Francis rejects proselytism four separate times in this interview. Francis declared: "Proselytism is solemn nonsense; it makes no sense."

Anti-Christ Francis is against educating unbelievers about our loving Almighty God. This is precisely what Satan wants Him to do. And so, he does it.

Below Statement released by the Vatican December 18, 2023

"The gospel is to sanctify everyone he said. of course, must be goodwill. And it is necessary to get precise instructions on the Christian life. It emphasizes that it is not the union that is blessed but the persons. But we are all sinners, why should we make a list of sinners who can enter the Church and a list of sinners who cannot enter the Church? This is not the gospel."

Yes, it is!

"Those who protest belong only to a small ideological group. I trust everyone will be reassured the spirit of this declaration which aims to include and not divide. It invites us to trust everyone as we trust in God."

The gospels say, Jesus Christ Himself, that the fundamental nature of mankind is fallen, sinful. To say to trust everyone opens the door to Satan completely! Promotes disbelief of Jesus Christ Himself. This is Satan talking.

In the above text Francis basically says that if you disagree then you are schematic.

The general reaction to the above is that when you bless two people you also bless the union between them. It is not possible to do otherwise.

Blessing LGBTQ marriages is indeed Satanic for it rejects the pronouncements of our Heavenly Father Himself.

This is not a magisterial document either. It is only the Pope Francis spouting off his personal wishes and proclamations.

Okay, I could go on and on with more and more examples of this wretched person we call the anti-Pope Francis. But I think you get the idea this man as our Blessed Mother Mary said is indeed the Anti-

Christ. And yes, he is here on the earth. And we indeed are living in the End of Times as prophesized by a lot of different Saints in the Bible and specifically our Blessed Mother Mary in other sections of this book.

Malachi Martin And the Satanic Infiltration of Impurity in The Church

March 1, 2024

Windswept House Vatican by Malachi-Martin

This book is a masterpiece. Father Martin did read the third secret of Fatima and felt all of God's sacred children needed to know its contents as spoken by our Blessed Mother Mary. He had taken an oath not to say anything. So, he used this book he called a "Faction" that reads like a novel but contains the actual facts of the Vatican's treachery surrounding the third secret of Fatima.

Keys of This Blood: Pope John Paul II Versus Russia and the West for Control of the New World Order by Father Malachi Martin

Father Malachi Martin was a Vatican insider and wrote about the untold story about the Vatican's role to establish and control in a one-world government.

The Widespread Theological Crime of The Vatican To Keep The Real Fatima Third Secret from God's Sacred Children

The Story of Sister Lucia of Fatima and The Vatican's Imposter Who Replaced Her

The third secret of Fatima has become a hotbed of controversy and manipulation. I started out writing a loving book about our loving

Blessed Mother Mary and her apparitions. Little did I know or anticipate I would run across such deceit, falsehoods, and manipulation I have uncovered during my investigations.

Before describing the third secret of Fatima. And before I present to you the exact and precise words that are Blessed Mother Mary has told me directly what the third secret of Fatima really is. I am forced to reveal to you a damned awful ugly thing that was perpetrated by the Catholic Church on Lucia of Fatima. The real Lucia is the girl on the right.

The premise is quite simple. Lucia it is an honest and loving Christian woman. She was spoken to by our Blessed Mother Mary back in 1917. She was told what was going to happen in the future. This included the high levels of the Catholic Church engaging in wretched practices of Satanic in nature. What you will read below is also motivation for the Church to make the real sister Lucia disappear, which they did.

As our Blessed Mother Mary says directly to me, when Pope Francis recently said the Anti-Christ is now on the earth, Blessed Mother said, "***he should know, because he is the Anti-Christ***." Please really think about our Mother's words. Pope Francis IS the Anti-Christ. WE ARE ALREADY IN THE END OF TIMES!

Lucia simply wanted to tell the world what Blessed Mother Mary told her. She refused to play along with what the Vatican wanted her to do! For that, she was cloistered away to an unknown convent not to be found or communicated with. Instead, an imposter woman replaced her. Below are the pictures of both women. Because of modern photographic facial recognition analysis, it became easy to detect and prove that the real Sister Lucia is not to be seen and replaced by another woman whose name we do not know.

Never in my worst nightmares would I have suspected such prominent levels of treachery as I have found.

Sister Lucia 1 and Sister Lucia 2

Dear sacred children of our Almighty Father, this next section is copied word for word from the Norvus Nordo Watch website. Full attribution is respectfully given to the fine Christians that make that website possible. The below article was published on March 26, 2019.

My personal feelings it is a sinister Satanic plot by people at various positions of trust and power in the Church. Hierarchy that plotted against all of us in the laity so as to do two things:

1. Deceive us to falsehood, false things against the true Lucia.

2. To hide this sinister truth about the Vatican and its Satanic role in the end of times.

I have been a Catholic Christian all my life and to find out garbage such as this makes me enraged and sick to my stomach. This treachery had to span multiple popes which makes things even worse in my eyes.

From ***"The Fatima Crusader, Issue 132, Spring 2024"***

Doctor Marion Horvat after speaking with both the original Lucia and the suspected impostor Lucia, he wrote, "sister Lucy appears solemn, composed, and reserved. She always stands in a very collected way, her hands in a discreet gesture. She appears to be a person unaccustomed to being photographed, a bit awkward and uncomfortable with it. From her postures, gestures, and expression, it is easy to believe she is the person who saw Our Lady and understood the gravity of the message and the role she should play in it.

The second Lucy, we see a person with a different state of spirit. She is always smiling at ease in public and relaxed in her postures and gestures. She has lost the natural timidity type of sister Lucia I. She became not only fearless but also completely comfortable and integrated in ambiences external to her contemplative life. Her face is smiling and jovial. She no longer seems anxious about the future, her mission, the coming chastisement, the corporation of consecrated souls, or the many other concerns she expressed before. She seemed optimistic and content.

Doctor Horvat concluded the differences in physical characteristics, mannerisms and testimonies of sister Lucia I and sister Lucia II suggested that the latter may be an impostor.

Doctor Chojnowski Concluded the following:

Facial mathematics reveals discrepancies in the ratios of nose with, mouth with, and interpupillary distances of the two subjects. Ratios

which normally remain constant throughout adulthood. Based on 6 independent ratios yielded by 7 facial lengths, a facial mathematician calculated that the probability Sister Lucy I and Sister Lucy II being the same person is one in approximately 13 million.

Now the text from this important article.

Sister Lucia 1 vs. Sister Lucia 2

We at Sister Lucy Truth publicly declare, based on evidence presented here. We've found it to be morally and scientifically certain the woman portrayed as "Sister Lucy," from her first public appearance in 1967, to her death in 2005, was not the same person as Sister Lucy. The Sister Lucy, Seer of Fatima and Visionary who predicted the Miracle of the Sun on October 13, 1917.

This, one of the greatest frauds in the History of the Church, was discovered through the use of the most sophisticated facial recognition programs. Along with the accumulated testimony of plastic surgeons, orthodontists, forensic artists, private investigators, handwriting analysts, and facial recognition experts.

Due to the availability of hundreds of photos of "Sister Lucy" available on the internet and in authoritative biographies, this case of substitution, fraud, and stolen identity has been able to be uncovered and analyzed. Without the judgment of the best and most relevant professionals available, we would not be making this grave accusation and presenting this charge.

We will continue to accumulate and post on this site new studies and research concerning this investigation as they are produced and published. All of the names of the relevant experts shall be published along with their professional findings. The truth of the disappearance of the true Sister Lucy and the identity of the imposter shall be placed before an internationally based private investigator who will investigate and solve the case.

The fraud has been identified and named. We charge the highest officials in the Vatican with conspiracy to perpetuate and conceal the substitution of Sister Lucy dos Santos of Fatima with an as yet unknown Imposter. [21]

I have felt that it is getting increasingly urgent to bypass the Catholic Church which has turned into nothing more than a stumbling block for the truth of things. I am also completely angered by Pope Francis for he is revealing Himself as an enemy of real Christians in my humble

---

[21] Malachi Martin: The Vatican Used a Fake Sister Lucia to Bury Fatima – RETURN TO TRADITION

opinion. He is attempting to drag secular socialist principles, progressive policies, and other reprehensible things like blessing same-sex marriages into our beloved Church. His lame excuse is that it is the two people involved in the relationship that are Blessed, not the relationship. Frankly how stupid does he think we are.

Pope Francis is also guilty of a dereliction of duty considering he purposely waited until the ninth year of His pontificate to consecrate Russia and Ukraine to your Immaculate Heart. (This was also proven to be a fraud as well) By then it was too late because Russia invaded Ukraine and there are many hundreds of thousands of dead people that should not have happened.

April 11, 2024

Question: Dear Mother Mary, have I misunderstood something in the previous few paragraphs?

Answer: *No, my son. Everything you said bothers me just as much as you did, probably even more. It has mightily challenged my patience regarding consecrating Russia and Ukraine into my peaceful Immaculate Heart.*

Pope Francis is trying to merge a socialist one world government politics with our Blessed Church that was founded by my dear son Jesus. The Church has been founded to be a wholly spiritual place of prayer and communion with your Almighty Father in Heaven. It is never ever meant to be a meeting place between spiritual love and human politics. But this is what has happened with Pope Francis. I too am angered regarding what he has done and failed to do.

My goal is simple. I want to finally once and for all tell the world what it is that should have been revealed in 1960 per your request. I will reveal it to the world by means of this extensive book and have it published and make it available everywhere. Also, my dear Mother, I'll speak to my publisher about placing advertisements in Catholic and Christian publications for this ever so important book about your apparitions. There will be emphasis on the third secret of Fatima as amplified by Akita. My publisher will also have it translated into many languages as I can afford to pay for it.

How I have spoken so much, and I want to listen to every word you tell me as it will be faithfully and lovingly put down into my computer.

February 27, 2024
Blessed Mother Mary said the following:

Dear son, you have no idea how much pleasure and happiness you bring to me. You're so joyful and wonderful in taking on what nobody else on earth has been willing to do. Your Father is right, you are so highly intelligent, and you are a fighter. It hurts me deeply when people of great faith shy away from telling the truth of things for such a wide variety of needless reasons.

I know you got very upset and angry by the Church refusing to tell God's sacred children the truth of things. I know that you understand this is because they do not want to as you would say rock their boat. You have great perceptive abilities as my son has told you many times when you wrote the first book God's Grand Design Of All Creation For Your Redemption. I know that what I am going to tell you will be published exactly as it is meant to be. This will take a lot of your energy, but you will do this because of your great love for the Trinity and me.

Recent Falsehoods from Pope Francis Regarding the Third Secret of Fatima

Dearest sacred children of our Heavenly Father, within my ongoing research efforts I have painfully discovered YouTube video that claims to reveal Pope Francis latest revelations regarding the third secret of Fatima. I was eating a hot dog at the time when the video played on my TV. After listening to what Pope Francis said about the third secret of Fatima, I wanted to squirt all my mustard on the screen. I am so sorry to say this, but Pope Francis is a Satanically controlled liar of horrific magnitude. The following are His exact words as presented by this YouTube video.

11

Pope Francis Lies About The 3ʳᵈ Secret of Fatima

The following text is spoken from Pope Francis Himself. Please pay close attention to what our so-called Pontiff describes as the so-called long awaited third secret of Fatima. Then please compare what our Blessed Mother Mary describes the third Sacred. Remember: It was Blessed Mother Mary back in October 1917 when she revealed the real truthful Fatima to Lucia, Francisco, and Jacinta. For the benefit of the entire world, Blessed Mary dictated her original words to Lucia in 1917 about the third secret of Fatima to be released to the world in 1960.

Pope Francis: "*The third secret of the Fatima reflects the breakout of wars and martyrdom and in some way, it seems Pope Francis has revealed some subtle truths about this third secret. He made it clear. As he declared World War three has already begun in piecemeal fashion. When he condemned the attack on Paris in November 2015. And again, in January 2023 when he made a call to stop to what was beginning to look like the start of WW III in different parts of the world.*

This clearly indicates the role of the Pope in the fulfillment of the third secret of Fatima. Cardinal Ratzinger rightly said, "the vision is an indicator of what we should do to force change in the right direction. This means it does not directly lay any emphasis on the role of a specific Pope such as Pope Francis in fulfillment of these prophesies. Rather it may reflect the role of the papacy through enforcing change a successive position as the world nears its end.

The prophecy reveals that the angels continue to cry penance beneath the arm of the cross. This reflects nothing truer than the number of Christian martyrdoms is on the rise. This evidence makes it clear that there is an ongoing war which may be different than what we have seen in the 1st and 2nd world wars. On separate occasions the Holy Father Francis has made reference to the global wars stating that it is happening in a piecemeal fashion. He charged His listeners with the need to stop the wars going all around us in places like Syria and Ukraine.

Just like it was shown in the third secret of Fatima he made it clear that wars hurts. Especially innocent young lives and old people. He shared the need that there is they need to stop the wars to make the world a safe and happy place to live in. In His charge, he pointed out the need to establish reforms for the needs of the people who are victim of wars for them to live happy lives again.

With these it is clear that the papacy is truly an agent of change in shaping a future for mankind as is revealed in the third secret. Now that the secret is revealed, what do we know about the fulfillment of other instructions of Our Lady?

After the third secret of Fatima, Lucia received another apparition from Mother Mary in 1929 where she received other parts of the secrets of Fatima.[22] It was during this appearance that Lucia received the need for Russia to be consecrated to the Immaculate Heart of Blessed Mother Mary. This revelation has led to continuous prayers requesting Mother Mary's intercession for the conversion of Russia. This was done in 1942 by Pope Pius during World War 2.[23] This continues to be a practice for succeeding popes including John Paul II and Pope Francis. The need and the urgency to pray the rosary for Russia was born from the rise of communist party. Which ultimately denied the existence of God and the period of Joseph Stalin's reign when he imprisoned and executed millions of people including Christians.

---

[22] *Blessed Mother Mary: I did not, I repeat I did not contact sister Lucia in 1929 and I did not instruct her regarding the consecration of Russia.*

[23] *When Pope Francis claimed that the consecration of Russia to my Immaculate Heart occurred through Pope Pius during World War II he was also lying. Remember our dear beloved son, Russia has yet to be consecrated to my Immaculate Heart even now as this wonderful book is being written in May of 2024.*

This consecration of Russia was at the Heart of the world's peace with the threat of annihilation which remained evident with the threat of Russia's nuclear weapons. When the Archbishop of Moscow visited Lucia, she asked Him if he was openly practicing in the city and when he said a falsehood yes. She said that this meant that the prophecy of Fatima had been fulfilled. Now the Archbishop has also shared that the statue of Our Lady of Fatima stands in every Church in His country. <u>With the fulfillment of this prophecy what does this mean for the fulfillment of the third secret?"</u>

<u>The Pope Told falsehoods! This Pope IS the Anti-Christ and The Third Secret of Fatima has NOT been fulfilled!</u> It describes in detail what is happening and will continue to happen until the return of Jesus Christ and His second coming!

The video host concludes with the following: Now that we have explored the Pope's position on the third secret of Fatima, what do you think about the third secret of Lucia and how it applies to our world.

The Words from Pope Francis. It contains pleasant words indeed. BUT! ALL OF IT IS A HERETICAL FALSEHOOD!

To this theological author there can be only one reason this nonsense would happen. It is because the Real Third Secret of Fatima contains terrible truths that implicate the Vatican in vast theological crimes against God's sacred children. Read onward dear people and you will find out what those crimes are as described word for word by our Blessed Mother Mary herself!

By the way, if I sound a bit angry about things it is because I am.

It must be noted that the previous paragraphs are ascribed directly to Pope Frances who describes in detail false facts about the Third Secret of Fatima. Now read below where he claims that there is "No Third Secret!"

May 10, 2024

Pope Francis said the following lie: **"No third secret of Fatima exists!"** [24]

My dear sacred children of Almighty God, if there is ever proof Cardinal Bergoglio AKA Pope Francis is an apostate, the anti-Christ and or heretic this is it. Along with the other heretical statements made by Him contained in other sections of this book, the absolute denial of the third secret of Fatima is the most outrageous, the most sinister and tyrannical.

Sister Lucia who wrote down precisely what our Blessed Mother Mary told her was threatened with death by the local Bishop in Portugal because she dared to write down the truth. That was the beginning of the Catholic Church doing everything it could to destroy the truth of what our Blessed Mother Mary wants to tell all of our Heavenly Father's sacred children.

You will find all the consequences of not listening to Blessed Mother Mary and her warnings both in the coverage in this book of Fatima and la Salette in addition to Akita. I hate to say it, but I am so enraged at this fake Pope if I were close to Him, I would slap Him for the damage he's attempting to do to God's sacred children.

I need to mention why Pope Francis is a fake pope. Simply put, it is directly due the mountain of heretical activities and policies he has enacted and wants to do more of them. He for example wants to merge our Beloved Catholic Church founded by Jesus Christ with many other religions like Buddhism, Hinduism, and Islam. It is in this way he destroys our Church by blending it into some bastardized thing none of us can recognize. Many cardinals and bishops are fighting against all this crap but so far have been unsuccessful. Pope Francis has cancelled or eliminated many God-centered people that have opposed him. This is why I call him a tyrant in other sections of this book.

His behavior, his dictator attitude canceling good honest faithful people in the Catholic hierarchy is proof he indeed is the Anti-Christ.

---

[24] Something Bad About Our Lady & Warned "No Real 3rd Secret of Fatima Exists, You're Told falsehood" (youtube.com)

These actions are exactly what Satan wants. Lastly, I must add combining Catholicism with other religions into one prepares mankind for a one-world government where it is now easy for Satan to take the throne over all of God's sacred children. Mother Mary speaks to this very point.

In Conclusion

I conclude this part of this booklet by restating "the Catholic Church is no longer what you think it is ". This does not mean you should not attend mass! We are talking about the highest levels in the Vatican and levels of cardinals and some bishops. Local churches still do a wonderful job of illuminating our biblical scripture. They do a magnificent job of providing the sacraments to all of us.

The best way to protect yourself from the constant disintegration from the top of the Catholic Church is to purchase a catechism that was printed more than 10 years ago. Why 10 years? Because 10 years ago is when cardinal Bergoglio became Pope. And when he started to negatively influence. Using his multiple tentacles in the church to sway them away from the pure loving doctrine. Doctrine intended and stated by our Lord and Savior Jesus Christ when he founded the Catholic Church, input St. Peter in the seat of the Pope.

The blessings of God and love to all of you.

Richard Ferguson, Author with our Blessed mother Mary without whom this booklet would never be possible.

APPENDIX

Christianity and the Vatican

Bishop Strickland's Warning to the Faithful: "There's A Storm Coming"

Bishop Strickland's Warning to the Faithful: "There's A Storm Coming" (youtube.com).

https://www.youtube.com/watch?v=vA32lzCJRwA

Bible flagged under new book ban. To think that Biblical literature is now getting more and more censored and illegal. This IS PART OF THE END OF TIMES

Bible flagged under new book ban law pushed by Republicans in Utah - YouTube

https://www.youtube.com/watch?v=TUCXmGeIBVc

Father Chad: this country is fulfilling end times prophecy.

ID833 SAL Gas Station YT DMZ SC162 Maor (youtube.com)

https://www.youtube.com/watch?v=nwPtLykImV8

Exposing the satanic infiltration of our church.

Exposing the SATANIC Infiltration of Our Church! With Dr. Janet Smith (youtube.com)

https://www.youtube.com/watch?v=LzNNtMvfXAo

New Details About Pachamama Show What Pope Francis Did Was Far Worse Than Anyone Realized . Return To Tradition.

https://www.bing.com/search?q=New+Details+About+Pachamam a+Show+That+What+Pope+Francis+Did+Was+Far+Worse&q s=n&form=QBRE&sp=-
1&lq=1&pq=new+details+about+pachamama+show+that+what +pope+francis+did+was+far+worse&sc=0-
73&sk=&cvid=FC47FF97C3BB4C15ADE29EC837AACBF2&ghs h=0&ghacc=0&ghpl=

Archbishop Vigano Responds to Francis' Diabolical Statement About Baptism. Return To Tradition
https://www.youtube.com/results?search_query=Archbishop+Viga no+Responds+To+Francis%E2%80%99+Diabolical+Statement +About+Baptism

Simply put, Cardinal Bergoglio wants to secularize the sacrament of baptism. I'm so angry about this one that perhaps our so-called Pope should just tell everyone go get a cup of tap water, pore over their head of the baby while saying these words "Yeah God."

Fatima's 3rd secret: Vatican's dark deception
Fatima's 3rd secret: Vatican's dark deception - YouTube
backward told you to
https://www.youtube.com/results?search_query=Fatama%27s+3rd +secret+%3A+Vatican%27s+dark+deception
The In-between
This video is the absolute best and most accurate source of the third secret of Fatima. It agrees with what our Blessed Mother has personally said to me in the past months. This information is to be cherished and studied. It is Godly truthfulness for your personal spiritual growth and all the others of our Heavenly Father's sacred children still on this earth.

Cardinal Burke denounces the godless ideology of the Synodal Church promoted by Pope Francis
https://www.youtube.com/watch?v=WxgxtSXfuV0

Father James Altman – Bergoglio is not the Pope, because he has proved he DOES NOT believe in basic Christianity.
https://www.youtube.com/results?search_query=Father +James+Altman+%E2%80%93+Bergoglio+is+not+the+Pope

The chilling revelation of a priest who read the third secret of Fatima intact.
https://www.youtube.com/results?search_query=The+chilling+revelation+of+a+priest+who+read+the+third+secret+of+Fatima+intact

Nuns smeared by bishops and the media for rejecting Francis.
https://www.youtube.com/results?search_query=Nuns+smeared+by+bishops+and+the+media+for+rejecting+Francis

The vortex - another persecuted priest
https://www.youtube.com/results?search_query=The+vortex+-+another+persecuted

Archbishop Vigano responds to Francis diabolical statement about baptism.
https://www.youtube.com/results?search_query=Archbishop+the+gunner+responds+to+Francis+diabolical+statement+about+baptism

Persecuted from within: a priest whistle-blower story.
https://www.youtube.com/results?search_query=Persecuted+from+within%3A+a+priest+whistleblowers+story

"Servants of Satan": archbishop Vigano responds to Pope Francis blessings for
https://www.youtube.com/results?search_query=Servants+of+Satan%3A+arch+Bishop+Vigano+responds+to+Pope+Francis+blessings+for

Pachamama meaning. It is a pagan goddess promoted by Francis.
https://www.youtube.com/results?search_query=pachamama+meaning
https://www.youtube.com/watch?v=8byD6EBF-4s

Pope Francis consecration to Pachamama
https://www.youtube.com/results?search_query=Pope+Francis+co
nsecration+to+pachamama

Francis sins the most wicked message about the Eucharist.
https://www.youtube.com/results?search_query=Francis+sins+the
+most+wicked+message+about+the+Eucharist

The Pope blew it big time when he said this.
https://www.youtube.com/results?search_query=The+Pope+Blew
+it+big+time+when+he+said+this

Did Francis just call Jesus a liar?
https://www.youtube.com/results?search_query=Did+Francis+just
+call+Jesus+a+liar%3F

The Pope is shocked: Medjugorje prophecy coming true in 2024!
Vatican alert
https://www.youtube.com/results?search_query=The+Pope+is+sh
ocked%3A+Medjugorje+prophecy+coming+true+in+2024!+Vat
ican+alert

people are already accepting the mark of the Antichrist without…
https://www.youtube.com/results?search_query=people+are+alrea
dy+accepting+the+mark+of+the+Antichrist+without%E2%80%
A6

Heresy of the Pope - John MacArthur
https://www.youtube.com/results?search_query=Heresy+of+the+P
ope+-+John+MacArthur
John MacArthur is a well-known televangelist who is a person that
sticks to the Bible. This is a good video to watch where he gives multiple
examples of Pope Francis and his anti-Catholic heretical teachings.

Pope Francis finally reveals the truth about the third secret of Fatima. NO, he did NOT. He lied about Fatima 3 distorting the truth into nice sounding lies.

https://www.youtube.com/results?search_query=Pope+Francis+fin ally+reveals+the+truth+about+the+third+secret+of+Fatima

Note: two things about this disgusting Vatican video - the picture of sister Lucia is a fake as covered within this book written by me and our Blessed Mother Mary. Pope Francis is a Satanic liar. Secondly, what he says is the third secret of Fatima IS NOT! The truth of the third secret is contained within the book you're holding in your hands. Among many prophecies contained in the authentic third secret of Fatima is the prophecy the 112th Pope will be the Antichrist. Cardinal Jorge Bergoglio IS the 112th Pope with the chosen name Francis!

Always remember, dear sacred child of our Heavenly Father, Pope Francis is the antichrist! And everything he says and does is aimed at one purpose, to destroy the Christian Church that was founded by our Lord and Savior Jesus Christ. He is attempting to create a second Church with the name Synod in it. I included this video so you can see firsthand the falsehoods that spew out of Bergoglio's Satanic mouth. If you sense I am angry about this, you're completely correct! So too is our Blessed Mother Mary!

Francis is purposefully trying to provoke faithful Catholics by insulting Mary.

https://www.youtube.com/results?search_query=Francis+is+purpo sefully+trying+to+provoke+faithful+Catholics+by+insulting+M ary

Francis gets political, smears faithful Catholics.

https://www.youtube.com/results?search_query=Francis+gets+poli tical%2C+smears+faithful+Catholics

Vigano: is Francis invalid Pope?

https://www.youtube.com/results?search_query=Vigano%3A+is+Francis+invalid+Pope%3FI

Francis Is Purposefully Trying to Provoke Faithful Catholics by ...
https://www.youtube.com/watch?v=hlFi-gT1Ok8
Return to Tradition

Anthony Stein a well-known and respected traditionalist within the Catholic Church, confirmed the people within the Vatican have published anti-Blessed Mother Mary material that is exposed in this video. This is how Satan works. Chip away at the foundational structure of our Blessed Church founded by our Lord and savior Jesus Christ, one brick at a time. And so, this is the latest chipping with the target being our Blessed Mother Mary.

The pope blew it big time when he said this.

https://www.bing.com/search?q=the+pope+blew+it+big+time+when+he+said+this&qs=n&form=QBRE&sp=-1&lq=0&pq=the+pope+blew+it+big+time+when+he+said+thi s&sc=1343&sk=&cvid=396179A9C5C54C4DB4ECEA6500000700&ghsh=0&ghacc=0&ghpl=

During this seemingly simple interview, the fake Pope Francis said things that contradict the core teachings of our Lord and savior Jesus Christ.

Pope Francis finally reveals the truth about the third secret of Fatima. No, he did not...just more lies.

https://www.youtube.com/live/6EjLpfSkb8Y

What the Pope just said in this video are damned, damned, damned falsehoods. The beauty of this book you hold in your hands is you have the word for word loving description directly from our Blessed Mother Mary. Each word, every single word that is contained in this book is exactly what our Blessed Mother Mary has said that Fatima number three really is. There can be no greater proof that so-called heretic Pope

Francis is under the direct control of Satan himself. I am so enraged with this, if I got close enough to our fake Pope, I would have an extremely tough time restraining myself from punching him in the nose!

This is so evil and clever at the same time very much like what Satan loves to do. First there is the admission that what has been said about Fatima since 1960 has been a falsehood. That in and of itself is disgraceful and a direct violation of Canon law about honesty and one of the ten commandments. The Vatican knows people did not believe that description they handed out calling it the third secret of Fatima. Mother Angelica of the EWTN TV program along with many others within the Catholic Church did not believe what the Vatican was pumping out as the third secret.

So, what did they do? They invented another bigger falsehood that simply replaces the previous falsehood calling it finally the truth is revealed. They are a bunch of Satanic bastards and should be stripped of all papal authority! GRRR!

For more information contact the publisher at
info@advbooks.com

*A*dvantage
BOOKS

Longwood, Florida, USA
we bring dreams to life™
www.advbookstore.com

www.ingramcontent.com/pod-product-compliance
Lightning Source LLC
LaVergne TN
LVHW051352080426
835509LV00020BB/3405